C000129000

EM&LO'S **SEX TOY**

EM&LO'S SEX
An A-Z Guide to
Bedside Access
BY EM&LO
ILLUSTRATIONS B

CHRONICLE BOOKS
SAN FRANCISCO

An A-Z Guide To

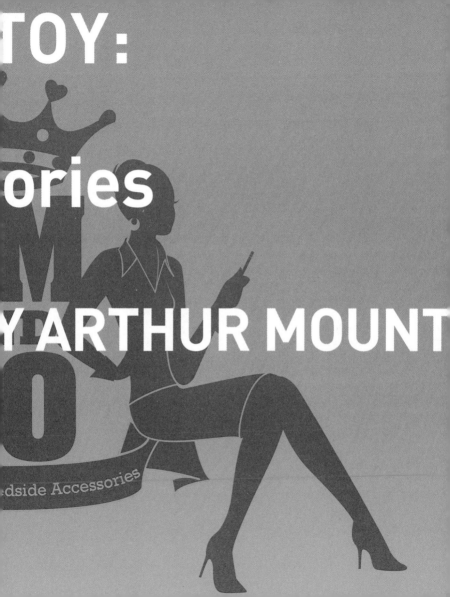

TEXT COPYRIGHT © 2006 BY
EMMA TAYLOR AND LORELEI SHARKEY.
ILLUSTRATIONS COPYRIGHT © 2006
BY ARTHUR MOUNT.

LIBRARY OF CONGRESS CATALOGING-IN-
PUBLICATION DATA:
TAYLOR, EMMA (EMMA JANE)
    EM & LO'S SEX TOY : AN A-Z GUIDE TO
    BEDSIDE ACCESSORIES / BY EM & LO.
    P. CM.
    INCLUDES INDEX.

ISBN-10: 0-8118-5283-0
ISBN-13: 978-0-8118-5283-8

1. SEX. 2. SEX CUSTOMS. 3. SEXUAL
EXCITEMENT. 4. SEX INSTRUCTION.
I. SHARKEY, LORELEI. II. TITLE.
    HQ21.T35 2006
    306.7—DC22

                2005030681

MANUFACTURED IN CANADA.

DESIGNED BY AYAKO AKAZAWA.
EM&LO LOGO DESIGNED BY
AYAKO AKAZAWA AND DAN SIPPLE.

DISTRIBUTED IN CANADA BY
RAINCOAST BOOKS
9050 SHAUGHNESSY STREET
VANCOUVER, BRITISH COLUMBIA V6P 6E5

10 9 8 7 6 5 4 3 2 1

CHRONICLE BOOKS LLC
85 SECOND STREET
SAN FRANCISCO, CALIFORNIA 94105

WWW.CHRONICLEBOOKS.COM

Acknowledgments

This book would not be possible without all the pros who patiently helped us navigate the vast sea of sex toys (and who gave us free shit): the nicest woman in the biz, Carol Queen, of GoodVibes.com and the Center for Sex & Culture; Robert Lawrence, also from the center; Coyote Days and Joyce Solano, also of GoodVibes.com; PR god Chuck Sanchez of the Berman Center; cool couple Dan and Shay Martin of Vibratex; materials girl Metis Black of TantusSilicone.com; friends Rebecca Suzanne and Anne Semans of Babeland.com; the very generous Denise of VixenCreations.com; prez Christophe of Blowfish.com; Ellen Barnard of A-Womans-Touch.com; Christian Trinker of FunFactory.de; Cory Silverberg of ComeAsYouAre.com; Kim Airs of GrandOpening.com; Natalia Daniel of MyPleasure.com; Peggy McIlnay-Moe of ElementalPleasures.com; Petra Zebroff of Libida.com; Jeff Rodman of Xandria.com; and Lori and Nicki of the now-defunct Extra Curious.

Thanks also to Rob and Joey, for being our guinea pigs; our sisters, for dishing the dirt; our agent, Ira Silverberg, for taking us seriously; and Jodi Davis, for being the smartest and most patient editor two advice ladies could hope for.

Toy Story

There was a time, long ago, when procuring a sex toy meant either visiting the produce department or going to a seedy store with a neon "XXX" in the window, curtained booths in the back that smelled mysteriously like chlorine, and a guy behind the counter with one good eye. You can thank pro-sex feminism, comprehensive sex education, Alfred Kinsey, Ernst Gräfenberg (of **G-spot** fame), Betty Dodson, *Sex and the City*, et al., for contributing to the mainstreaming of sex toys.

These days, countless online retailers offer bedside props safely, securely, and discreetly (i.e., plain paper packaging and generic billing details on your credit card statement). Gone are the days of the humiliating face-to-face handover of cash for a **Fleshlight**. Even **Drugstore.com** sells sex toys! (And we're not just talking about those **"back" massagers**—they stock dildos and all!) The in-person shopping experience has been transformed, too, by beautifully designed and inviting toy emporiums where people can ask questions and get honest, educated answers about sexual health and exploration without feeling like they need to wash their hands thirty-seven times when they get home. Couples are even making a trip to their little sex shop on the corner part of an evening out.

It's about freakin' time. Sure, **dildos** have been around since at least 10,000 B.C., and doctors were using **vibrators** to cure women of **"hysteria"** back in the nineteenth century, but it's only in the last decade or so that people have finally started to chill out and consider toys part of a healthy sex life. In 1994, the fourteenth World Congress of Sexology, an international gathering of sexuality scientists, declared, "Sexual pleasure, including autoeroticism [masturbation], is a source of physical, psychological, intellectual, and spiritual well-being." Ten years later, Durex's annual international sex survey found that more than a third of women own a vibrator or an "intimate massager." And a nationwide study by Chicago's **Berman Center** found that women who use vibrators experience higher levels of sexual desire, higher levels of sexual satisfaction, and higher rates of success in achieving orgasm. Hot *day-umm*. Toys aren't just for the ladies, though, and they're more than just a "widow's comforter," too. The same study found that women in relationships were even more likely to use sex toys than single gals.

Before this sexual awakening, the sex-toy industry was a "push" market, driven entirely by the manufacturers and distributors. The businesses were run *by* men and marketed *to* men, without much thought to women's bodies or real pleasure. But over the past decade, women—who, after all, are the ones who benefit most from toys—have managed to turn the industry into a "pull" market. By putting their money where their naughty bits are, female consumers have encouraged manufacturers to invest in research and development, place quality over quantity, and listen to their complaints (at least, when old-fashioned shame hasn't kept them from piping up about defective products). Hence, sex toys have gotten a *lot* better—for everyone.

"**Boy toy**" no longer means just a blow-up doll and a vat of Crisco. **Vibrators** are now designed with the **clitoris** in mind. **Dildos** have the **G-spot** on the brain. **Novelties** have taken a backseat to **high-end sex toys** and ergonomic, body-**contoured** vibes. **Lubes** got better. **Condoms** got thinner. **Glass dildos** can now pass as abstract art on your coffee table. Some of the most popular sex toys don't bear the slightest resemblance to a penis (no offense, guys, but it's not always about the dick). A **miniature vibrator** attached to a cock **ring** offers women vibrating clitoral stimulation during intercourse. Starter **strap-on** kits mean women across the country are saying, "**Bend over, boyfriend**." **Bachelorette-party paraphernalia** has been replaced by toys that actually get the job done.

The problem is, it's still a jungle out there, no thanks to states such as Alabama and Texas, which continue to honor outmoded laws banning the sale of sex toys (which they deem obscene). Given this country's puritanical tendencies, it shouldn't come as a surprise that the sex-toy industry is entirely unregulated, and many less-than-upstanding companies continue to take advantage of this fact. The most benign effect is that the market is still flooded with cheap, crappy, gimmicky toys about as likely to get you off as an episode of *Larry King Live*. They're often made in China, most likely under dubious labor conditions. And since they're billed as **novelties**, they don't come with instructions for safe use or care. More troubling, it means many toys on the shelves are made of potentially carcinogenic **materials** (see **phthalates**), and because there's no organization overseeing safety and package labeling, you'd never know it.

That's where this book comes in—it explains why you should use sex toys, which toys you should check out, where you can buy them, and how you can use them. We even tell you how to introduce a toy to a hesitant partner (see **communication**) and how to hide your toy collection from a nosy aunt (see **storage**)! We have personally tried just about every sex toy reviewed in this book—and, where that wasn't possible, for obvious anatomical reasons, we interviewed someone who has. (You should have seen the brawl that almost broke out over which one of us got to test-drive the **Rock Chick vibrator**.)

A word on how to shop with this book: There is a dizzying array of online sex-toy retailers out there. Most appeal to more prurient interests and are unhelpful and ill informed. They tell you what they think you want to hear ("She'll be writhing and moaning all night long!" or "It'll make her pussy virgin-tight again!") rather than what you need to know (like, oh, say, that a toy might cause friggin' *cancer* if you don't whack a condom on it). They regurgitate unhelpful package copy. They sell "**porn-star** pussies." In short, they do everything that the XXX neon stores do, just online. And we think you should avoid them like the clap.

So we singled out some online sex-toy retailers we like very much—represented by the initials you see after each toy mentioned in this book. We'd trust these stores with our genitals *and* our credit card information. For the most part, we avoided the Wal-Mart-esque biggies, such as the original AdamandEve.com—we find they leave us a little cold. Whether you're a man or a woman, gay or straight, we believe that the smaller stores with a more feminine approach (whether they're owned and operated by women or not) will give you a better shopping experience.

The best six of the bunch are **GoodVibes.com** (GV), **Babeland.com** (BL), **A-Womans-Touch.com** (WT), **Blowfish.com** (BF), **MyPleasure.com** (MP), and **Libida.com** (LB). The first three in this list have bricks-'n'-mortar stores you can visit, too, which is great for getting a sense of a toy's size, vibration strength, noisiness, beauty, etc. But when that's not convenient or geographically possible, their online stores will do just fine. We've also found **Drugstore.com** (DS) to be helpful for well-priced mainstream stuff, **ErosBoutique.com** (EB) and **ExtremeRestraints.com** (EX) for **BDSM** paraphernalia, **ComeAsYouAre.com** for Canucks, and **Xandria.com** (XA) for price comparison and gimmicky-but-worth-it items. You can even buy high-quality **silicone** dildos directly from one of the best manufacturers in the biz at **VixenCreations.com** (VC). And when we say a toy is "available almost everywhere," we mean it's stocked at most of the aforementioned stores—we don't mean that you can pop down to the nearest Duane Reade and pick it up. One day, though . . .

By the way, many mom-and-pop sex toy shops aren't online like the stores we mention here but are just as friendly, responsible, and affordable. So, check out your local alternative newspaper to see whether there's one in your town. If there is, consider it your civic duty to support it!

We've included price ranges for most toys: "$" means less than $20, "$$" means $20-$60; "$$$" means $60-$100; and "$$$$" means $100-$200. For anything more expensive than that (a.k.a. **bedroom bling**), we've included the actual price. Prices can vary significantly from store to store, so shop around for the best deal. And by "best deal," we mean the lowest price on that particular toy, not some cheap knock-off made in China. At first glance, you may think many of the toys we've included are quite pricey. But though high cost doesn't necessarily *guarantee* high quality, in this industry you usually get what you pay for: Cheap toys are typically made cheaply out of cheap materials. High-quality sex toys are an investment in the quality of your sexual pleasure and satisfaction. You probably wouldn't think twice about spending $50, even $100, on a nice meal or a new pair of jeans; aren't your genitals worth that same investment?

As a general rule, we've found Blowfish.com's prices to be significantly lower on most products—but it's also a bitch of a site to navigate. GoodVibes.com and Babeland.com tend to be pricier, but they both have a special place in our hearts (and pants). And though A-Womans-Touch.com may have less of a selection, you're guaranteed to get products deemed safe by their chemist (he's tested every single toy they sell). If you're toy shopping for the first time, we suggest starting with these three and then price shopping once you're more familiar with what's out there. And, hey, you might decide you feel so comfortable at GoodVibes.com or Babeland.com or A-Womans-Touch.com that you buy there, too. You're paying for the entire shopping experience, and, when it comes to sex toys, that counts for a lot.

If you have trouble locating an item reviewed in this book, it's because stores are constantly updating their inventory, replacing toys with items they consider an improvement on an earlier model, and renaming toys because they came up with something catchier. In fact, only a handful of toys—usually the most famous ones, such as the **Hitachi Magic Wand**—appear under the same name in every location. The **Lumina Wand**, on the other hand, has at least six names! We've made an effort to cross-reference various names to clue you in, but it can still be pretty damn confusing. If you can't figure it out, ask a sales assistant, either in person or by e-mail. (And if no one will help you, take your business elsewhere.)

One more point of business: If a word or phrase is bolded, either in this introduction or anywhere else in the book, that means it has its very own entry in the encyclopedia. This may require a bit of flipping back and forth the first few times you open the book, but pretty soon you'll pick up the lingo and won't need to turn back thirty pages to figure out what the hell it means for a toy to be **monogamous**.

Despite this fancy system, our encyclopedia is in no way exhaustive. If it were, it would be longer than *War and Peace* and we'd still be road-testing vibes into our seventies (though, for the record, we plan on doing that regardless of our publishing schedule). It's simply an introduction to the world of toys. We reviewed best-selling toys, our favorite toys, toys that cracked us up, toys our friends in the biz raved about, toys our favorite retailers consider sleepers, the toys we lost our vibratory cherry to, etc. But *your* favorite toy might not even be in this book. Your clitoris or your starfish or your nipples or your balls aren't swayed by best-seller lists, and they don't particularly care which toy Charlotte from *Sex and the City* used, either. (Though we did, of course, review the **Rabbit Habit vibrator**, too.) It's okay to like a toy because it's pretty or because it's got a funky light display—after all, that's part of the experience. But bear in mind that some of the ugliest toys out there (like, say, the **Eroscillator**) boast legions of fans who evangelize with Scientology-esque fervor for their vibe of choice.

So, have at it. First, be sure to read the entries on **materials**, **cleaning & care**, and **storage**, as well as the important safety appendix in the back. Then, start with **beginner toys**. Try to buy toys manufactured in North America, Japan, or Europe. Don't forget to pick out a **lube** that complements your toy (because some may destroy it). If you're not sure what a toy is made of, put a **condom** on it. Keep spare batteries on hand, because nothing kills a sex-toy moment like the dying wail of your little motor running out of juice. Get a toy for your **bath**, for your **butt**, for your best friend (see our entry about gift-giving **etiquette**). Get another one for yourself. And another. Remember, whoever dies with the most sex toys wins!

Key to Abbreviations

BF = Blowfish.com
BL = Babeland.com
DS = Drugstore.com
EB = ErosBoutique.com
EX = ExtremeRestraints.com
GV = GoodVibrations.com
LB = Libida.com
MP = MyPleasure.com

VC = VixenCreations.com
WT = A-Womans-Touch.com
XA = Xandria.com
$ = under $20
$$ = $20-$60
$$$ = $60-$100
$$$$ = $100-$200

A

acrylic

Faux **glass** made of transparent **plastic, hard**. Lucite is a popular brand of acrylic. Sex toys made of it are hard, **nonporous**, and as smooth as a baby's bottom frozen solid. They are crack and shatter *resistant*, but you *can* break them (as we found out after dropping a **Lumina Wand** on the floor twenty times). So, if you've got one with a crack, throw it away—you wouldn't want it breaking off inside you (plus, bacteria could get in a hairline fracture). Acrylic toys are most often **pelvic-floor-muscle** strengthening tools and **G-spot** dildos—i.e., when your primary focus is having something rock hard to grip onto. And we mean *rock* hard, not the kind of hyperbolic "oh, baby, you're rock hard" that refers to nonacrylic, real-life dongs, especially in movies with titles such as *Between a Rock and a Hard-On*. Acrylic is also **phthalate** free (yay!), but it can't be sterilized by boiling in water, like **silicone** (eh).

To **clean** an acrylic toy, simply give it a good scrub with antibacterial soap and water. If you clean with a bit of elbow grease (i.e., you're not the type to leave scraps of congealed casserole on "clean" dishes in the drying rack), you can use acrylic toys without condoms. Just to be on the safe side, though, we recommend always using condoms if you plan on sharing a toy. Seriously, folks, is it that much to ask that you buy one toy per partner if you want to go condom free? FYI, if your acrylic toy comes with a raised seam or any bumps left over from the casting process, use a **nail file** to smooth them away before use.

addiction

Compulsive physiological and/or psychological dependence on one's favorite sex toy. This condition can be observed in the *Sex and the City* episode in

→

which Charlotte buys a Rabbit (see **Rabbit Habit & Rabbit Pearl vibrators**) and consequently never wants to leave her apartment and Carrie and Miranda are forced to hold an intervention. (We were always a little disturbed by how comfortably they handled Charlotte's vibrator when they knew *exactly* where it had been.)

Women commonly worry that they will become addicted to their toys, unable to experience the same pleasure with their nonrobot partners. Men commonly worry that they can't compete with robots. But as long as a woman mixes it up and is willing to try new things, with and without toys, there's nothing wrong with reaching for a battery-powered friend every now and then. It's true, some women find they can reach orgasm only with the intense vibrations from a machine—but this is not addiction; it's simply an individual anatomical imperative. And we'd say machine-assisted orgasms are better than no orgasms at all. Men should be comforted by the fact that most women know a **vibrator** cannot pay her compliments or cuddle with her. *Male* addiction is much less common due to the fact that the basic formula for his orgasm is typically much simpler than hers (insert, thrust, repeat). However, in rare cases, the severely socially awkward have been known to fall for their **Real Doll**. Such creepy obsession was the subject of the low-budget, so-horrendously-bad-it's-*almost*-good, soon-to-be-cult-classic *Love Object* (2003). See also the Safety Tips Appendix.

adult entertainment

Videos, DVDs, skin rags, live shows, Web sites—pretty much anything **X-rated** that did, actually, mean to turn you on. So, super-steamy R-rated French cinema doesn't really count. But everything from soft-core "Skinemax" features such as *The Pleasure Zone 13* up to hardcore gonzo titles like—

→

warning to the faint of heart!– *Cum Guzzlers* (featuring women slurping ejaculation out of dog bowls) *does* count. About 99.9 percent of adult entertainment is plagued by at least three of the following: fake titties; bad dye jobs; dialogue that makes *One Life to Live* sound like *Annie Hall*; a disturbing lack of foreplay; a disturbing lack of pubic hair; mysterious stains on the packaging (if it's a rental); mullets.

Altoids

The "curiously strong mint" with sexy ad tag lines ("Pleasure in pain," "These mints have not yet been rated," "Shrinkage may occur," "Dental Damn!") that was the subject of a widely circulated 1997 e-mail extolling the mints' powers as an oral sex aid. (Hmmmm, we wonder who originally sent that e-mail? Could it be . . . *Altoids?!*) The faux e-mail reached widespread urban legend status when it was referenced in that noted collection of hot erotica, Kenneth Starr's impeachment report: Monica Lewinsky handed the prez a printout of the e-mail while she herself was sucking on an Altoid (cheeky monkey). The jury's still out on whether it's all hype. Do your own research, whether with Altoids, Tic Tacs, Fisherman's Friend, Hall's Mentholyptus, or Oral Fixation (hipster mints in a chic cigarette case), and report back. See also **edible accessories**.

anal beads, about

Anal beads look like a snapped-together kids' plastic necklace– the kind you can win in a gumball machine. In other words, totally *unlike* something you should stick in your beehind. But they feel rilly, rilly good, both on the way in and on the way out. The pros say you should insert the string slowly, one bead at a time, pausing for permission after each bead like a dirty game of Mother May I? Then pull the beads out (gently →

but not as slowly) either just before, or at, the moment of orgasm. Do not—repeat, do not—yank the beads out: This is not an area where you want rug burn. (Just the phrase "anal chafing" makes us clench.)

The cheapie kind of anal beads are attached on a nylon cord and made of plastic—so make sure you smooth down any rough plastic seams first (owee!) using a **nail file**. And be warned: That cord is going to get *nasty* after only three or four uses. So we'd say throw down a bit more money and go for high-quality beads built on a stalk of the same material (instead of on a string), like the **Flexi Felix**. This kind of toy is sturdier and easier to clean, especially if it's made of **silicone**, like our friend Felix. A more affordable option is **jelly**—see **anal beads, jelly** following—but then you'll have to contend with possibly toxic **phthalates**. And remember, as with any anal toy: **Lube** is your friend (the one you *have* to play with, 'cause your mother said so).

anal beads, jelly

These are **jelly**-rubber **anal beads** on a jelly-rubber stalk. The gradual escalation in size makes them good for nervous nellies: The smallest bead is ¼ inch in diameter, and the sizes build up to the largest, still a modest 1 inch around. The large bendy ring at the top gives you something to pull on when you sense your partner is rounding that final bend—or if they scream, "Enough already!"—though, as with any anal toy, jelly beads should always be removed steadily and smoothly: No matter the emergency, a jerky yank is always a bad idea. If the house is on fire, for example, just leave the beads in place while you find the nearest emergency exit.

Because jelly is **porous** and contains **phthalates**, they should always be used with a condom, though admittedly this can be a little awkward. If you insist on bareback beading, the toy should at least be a **monogamous** sex toy. (But, honestly, you're better off springing for a more expensive **silicone** version such as the **Flexi Felix** so your condom-free poking can be worry free, too.) Wash the jelly ones in soap and water after use. Available as Blue Beads on BL, as X-10 Beads on MP, or as the Grapes of Writhe on BF ($).

anal beads, silicone

See **Flexi Felix**.

anal play

According to **TantusSilicone .com**, one of the biggest trends in sex-toy sales right now is consumers' interest in the ass. Anal play is any sexual stimulation, external or internal, of the anus. The area is chock-full of nerves, so attention in the form of vibration or penetration can be very pleasing, as long as you do it correctly—and you're not some sexist, homophobic clean freak. Prepare for any incoming objects by getting plenty of fiber in your diet, dropping the kids off at the pool, taking a *thorough* shower, and maybe even orgasming first to loosen everything up down there. Wash any probes before and after use (because microscopic fecal bacteria can cause infection). In fact, use a condom to help keep things tidy and **STD** free.

Any toy you take spelunking should have a flared base, so it won't get lost up there, and should not be breakable. Obvious, right? Think again. Not all those emergency-room

→

stories are urban legends—a nurse friend of ours has personally relieved patients of, among other things, a **slimline vibrator**, a TV remote control, and a can of Axe Body Spray. Best to stick with the soft, bendy, size-appropriate toys made specifically for the tush. Start off small and work your way up: There's no such thing as a 12-inch Colon Pounder Starter **Kit**.

The asshole is not self-lubricating, so you've got to use **lube**—see **lubes, water-based** for products that won't degrade latex, unlike Crisco and other oils. Never force anything in there, and don't pull anything out like you're tugging on a goddamn emergency brake, either. TLC is key. Read *Anal Pleasure & Health,* by Jack Morin, for more deets.

Also, see the index for a comprehensive list of anal toys featured in this book. For nontoy, anal-related info, see **gerbils**, **P-spot**, and **perineum**.

Aneros butt plug

Actually, make that the Aneros Prostate Stimulator. No, seriously: This best-selling white plastic medical device was invented by a bunch of scientists to help relieve congested **prostate** fluid (sexy, we know). But it didn't take Aneros long to figure out that dudes with prostate problems were *really* enjoying their prescribed treatment (can you imagine the conversations at golf clubs across the country?), so now it's sold for health *and* pleasure. And, actually, even if your prostate has a clean bill of health, it can always benefit from a good massage. Plus, regular use of this baby can tone a guy's **pelvic floor muscles**, giving him more control over his orgasm (see **kegels**).

The Aneros plug basically surrounds his territories down there, stimulating his prostate internally and externally. It's got three parts: ❶ The insertable plug part curves slightly to hit his prostate and is 1 inch by 4 inches, about the size of a rather large man's thumb (though it's not just for men who fantasize about a large man's thumb in the bum). ❷ The wide, flat handle rests pleasantly against his **perineum**. ❸ The curlicue handle is used for insertion and removal, and nestles between his butt cheeks during use (cute, huh?). And here's the genius part: It's totally controlled by the ass muscles! We, er, shit you not. As he relaxes and contracts down there, the plug shifts a little, gently massaging the prostate as it goes. Look, ma, no hands! That said, the wearer, or his partner, can also use the curlicue handle to rock the plug back and forth to help things along. (By the way, women can get in on the Aneros, too; in their case, the handle will dip into the **vagina**.)

Once it's in, the rest is up to you. As with any **anal play**, don't forget to use lots of **lube**– any kind with this toy–and expect Aneros to feel a little *uninvited* for the first few minutes after insertion. Some men claim they can come from the Aneros alone, though they do admit this requires Sting-like concentration and dedication, at least the first few times. Others, like our guinea pigs, prefer to wear it while rubbing one out or having sex, which can result in "super-intense orgasms." And more than one user quoted on Aneros.com reported an uncontrollable desire to "growl." (Remember, kids, we don't laugh at other people's orgasms.) Sure, the Aneros is a little more expensive than your average butt plug, but **boy toys** that actually work are rarer than a TofuPup at a NASCAR race. Besides, doesn't your guy *deserve* a custom-built, patented poker?

→

The Aneros is **nonporous** and should be washed with mild soap and water. Sold by name most everywhere ($$). Buy it on Aneros.com, and the original design (there are new shapes) comes with a ninety-day money-back guarantee.

aphrodisiac

Any food or drink item rumored to put you in the mood, including oysters, truffles, strawberries, dark chocolate, Spanish Fly, Slippery Nipples, ecstasy, and a slice of pizza at just the right time. Scientists have never been able to prove their efficacy (and you can bet your chocolate-covered strawberries they tried), but the placebo effect is not to be underestimated. Aphrodisiacs are employed mostly by men in shiny suits who think playing a Marvin Gaye CD will get them laid. They will typically serve up their aphrodisiac of choice with a wink and a "sexy" grin. On a side note, some women have been known to serve a potential luvver food of a certain, um, texture—oysters, say, or the mystery dish at dim sum—to ascertain his comfort level with cunnilingus. However, any man who refers to his oral prowess while sucking a Blue Bay oyster off its shell is to be regarded with the highest suspicion. Subtlety, dudes: It's underrated. See also **edible accessories**.

Aqua Arouser waterproof vibrator

This multispeed **waterproof** vibe is a very strong swimmer. Admittedly, it's not exactly an **undercover** operator, like the **Duckie waterproof vibrator**, but some of us like our sex toys to look like they were built for grown-ups. This **vibrator** is fairly slim (1¼ inches across) and the clear **jelly** shaft is what they call in the biz "realistically veiny" (we wish there were a sexier way to say that), for added sensation. In addition, the Aqua Arouser features a cluster of nubbins (now *there's* a name for a candy bar) at its base to gently stimulate the **clitoris**. Because the AA is made of jelly (i.e., contains **phthalates**), keep your toy **monogamous** and to be extra safe, cover it in a **condom**. MP is the only place you can get it in aqua, though LB sells it in blue as the Water Willy, and BL has a longer, wider one called the Sparkle Splasher, with—you guessed it—pink sparkles! ($$)

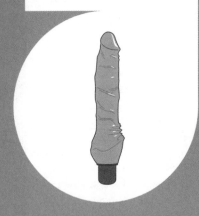

Audi-Oh butterfly vibrator

If you like doing it to music, this vibe's for you. A **miniature vibrator**—connected by cord to a battery pack about the size and weight of a brownie (with nuts)—is held in place by a **butterfly harness**. The vibe is built to respond to sound, creating an infinitely variable range of vibrations, instead of a boring, repetitive pattern or continuous vibration (though you can adjust the controls to give you just that). You can wear it in public (preferably *under* your clothes) to dance clubs, concerts, or your Abnormal Psych seminar. You can also input sound directly from audio devices like a portable CD player or your **iPod**, but you'll need a ⅛-inch audio cable and a Y adapter (that thingamajiggy that turns one output hole into two). And, to get the bullet in and out of the butterfly easily, you'll need a little water-based lube (also not

➜

included). Great for tech geeks and music fascists. It's worth getting one just so you can hear a new song and say, "It's got a good beat, and you can come to it." Available most everywhere, including Audi-Oh.com ($$$, not including the nine-volt battery you'll need). See also **remote control toys**.

Babeland.com (BL)

"Maybe we need a National Strap-On Association: It's easier to get a gun than a dildo in most parts of the country." So say Rachel and Claire, owners of the sex-toy retailer formerly known as Toys in Babeland (last year they got a new look for their Web site, a new logo, and an easier-to-remember name: Babeland.com). With a great online shop chock-full of merch and helpful sex ed, plus two funky stores in N.Y.C. (the Soho location is the best), one in Seattle, and one in L.A., Babeland is second only to **Good Vibes** in the sex-toy race, which means BL can get away with charging a bit more than most of its competitors. Its only exclusives are Babeland-branded condoms, lube, a vibrating flashlight key chain (the Babelight), and a Babeland Silver **Bullet**; the company prefers to focus on generating original sex ed content while letting the manufacturers do what they do best. Babeland is women owned and operated, like GV, and its sensibility is a little more urban, a little more rock 'n' roll. In other words, Babeland would be the sex store featured on Showtime's *The L Word*.

baby wipes

Once you get over the slightly seedy feeling of using a baby product for sex, you'll realize what an ingenious invention these things are. Use them to wipe off a sex toy immediately after use, or grab one after a facial or any kind of anal exploration. (A note to lazy fuckers: They're no substitute for a good scrub with soap before and after your sesh.) Discretion would suggest that you not keep them prominently displayed on your nightstand, though within arm's reach (perhaps in your "party drawer") is a nice touch. And good taste would suggest that you purchase a brand that

doesn't feature a snuggle-butt baby on its packaging—try Cottonelle Pre-Moistened Wipes (flushable, portable, and alcohol free, though they do contain fragrance). Three cheers for a new way to kill the rain forests! A.k.a. intimacy wipes.

bachelorette- party paraphernalia

Sashes, tiaras, boas, "Wild Girls" caution tape, plastic ball and chain, "naughty" confetti, "pin the hose on the fireman" games, poseable male pinups, Jell-O shots, "diamond ring" shot glasses, pecker straws, glow-in-the-dark penis-shaped to-go cups, "cocksucker" lollipops, condoms-on-a-stick, 4-foot inflatable willies, pecker party horns, penis balloons, penis candy rings, penis Mardi Gras beads, penis tattoos, penis straws, penis strobe pins—we could go on. See also **edible accessories**, **gag gifts**, and **novelties**.

bachelor-party paraphernalia

Strippers.

"back" massagers

Remember back in the seventies, when you used to go over to your friend Samantha's house to play, and on special days she would say, "Wanna see my mom's back massager?" And you kind of knew there was something secret about this back massager because of how well it was hidden (and what it was hidden *with*), and you and Samantha would take turns holding it on each other's backs. And then there was that one time when Samantha went downstairs to get more apple juice and Oreos, and you had the serendipitous idea to hold it on your happy place (you barely even knew you had a happy place back then), and after that Samantha became your Best Friend Forever.

Decades later, back massagers are still selling like hotcakes, providing external genital stimulation to women who've never experienced a day of back pain in their lives. In fact, the **Hitachi Magic Wand** is the most popular vibrating sex toy in the world—and yet the packaging features a leotard-clad, squeaky-clean housewife tending to her aching back and shoulders. While back massagers may not be as sexy or cute as all the custom-made sex toys out there, they hold a special place in our hearts (okay, they hold a special place in Em's pants). And, hey, some people *like* that whole medical-product vibe: It makes them feel less trashy, and it's easier to explain when your kid and her best friend discover it in your drawer. Let us count the ways we love back massagers: You can purchase one at a drugstore (DS; $$), you don't have to worry about going through airport security, back massagers tend to be sturdier and longer lasting than a lot of plastic novelty vibes, and, next time you get a

→

B

real backache after a grueling transatlantic flight, presto!—you own a back massager! Other popular back massagers include the **Wahl vibrator** and the Essential Multi-Massager (the latter is available almost everywhere; BL calls it the Essential Vibrator and GV names it the Essential Coil; $$).

ball gags

For advanced players only, and in particular for those players who take their sex play *very* seriously. A ball gag consists of a ball, usually made of **rubber** or **silicone**, with straps attached at either side to hold it in place—*in your mouth.* You know, like what Bruce Willis and Ving Rhames had in their mouths when they woke up in the basement with the **Gimp** in *Pulp Fiction.* The ball sits behind your teeth, and the straps go around your head. Variations on this theme include gags with a nubbin in the basic shape of a penis head, O-ring gags or metal dental contraptions that force

the mouth open, muzzles, pony bits, and masks or hoods that cover the mouth. Gags come in handy if you want to turn your **BDSM** play up to eleven, or if you're role-playing a kidnapping scenario and your "kidnapper" has a bit of a Quentin Tarantino thing. If you're prone to the giggles at the slightest spank or hint of dirty talk, however, a gag is not for you. Needless to say, you're not supposed to wear this for extended periods of time (it can seriously irritate the joints in your jaw), nor do we suggest donning one if you've got a stuffy nose or there's even the slightest chance your mom might walk in on you. Visit EB and EX for some *serious* examples ($-$$$). See also **restraints**.

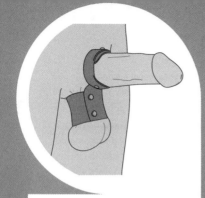

ball stretchers

A strip of material, usually attached to a cock **ring**, that pushes the testicles down deeper into the scrotal sac and pulls them away from the penis and body, with the intention of making them feel more vulnerable, exposed, and/or sensitive. There may also be another strap that separates each ball or a D-ring to which weights or leashes can be attached. Good if you prefer your testicles to look like two balloons about to pop rather than two balloons that have been deflated quite a bit (EX; $-$$$). See also **BDSM**.

bath accessories

We know of no better foreplay than a bubble bath, whether solo or à deux. If you're one of those corporate busy bees who finds it hard to shut down at the end of the day, try substituting a bath for all that mindless TV you've come to rely on. Light some **candles**, play some music, and leave the freakin' Blackberry in the kitchen. We like the bath products from the **Kama Sutra** line or V'Tae (BF), but, really, whatever floats your bath toys is fine (though if it's patchouli oil, we don't want to know). If you or your partner has a sensitive veegee, avoid overly fragranced products. Aveda products are pricey, but they're all-natural, so they're often a good fit with easily irritated private parts.

If you find yourself getting sleepy, administer a rubdown with a vibrating sponge (BL, MP, XA; $) or a vibrating shower scrunchie (LB; $), or just invite your **Duckie waterproof vibrator** into the tub. If you've

B

→

got company, check out the book *Hot & Steamy: Erotic Baths for Two*, by Annalise Witberg, for some saucy suggestions—it's waterproof, so you can actually read it in the bath, *and* it's designed to fit in your soap dish! Or, for some wet and wild erotic fiction, whether alone or with a friend, try the adults-only waterproof book *Aqua Erotica*.

But here's the rub (or, rather, the rope burn): Being *squeaky* clean means bath or shower water will wash all your natural lube away, and regular water-based lubes will slide right off, too. You're going to need some waterproof (i.e., silicone) **lube** if you're planning on doing more than just washing behind your ears.

If you think squeaky clean is overrated, enlist the help of some **edible accessories**—basically, an excuse to put your mouths all over each other. Just be sure to eat all your veggies at dinner first. Because you're already in the shower, cleaning up the leftovers will be a cinch.

BDSM

Overlapping acronym for one, two, or all three of the following types of kinky play: bondage and discipline, domination and submission, and sadism and masochism (or sadomasochism). Though there are certainly members of BDSM communities who take their kink *very* seriously, you don't need to know any secret handshakes or Trekkie lingo to dabble in power play using BDSM paraphernalia, such as **ball gags**, **blindfolds**, **bondage belts** and **tape**, **candle wax**, **canes**, **collars**, **cuffs**, **gimp suits**, **nipple clamps**, nylon **rope**, **paddles**, role-playing outfits, **spreader bars**, and **whips** (see **kinky toys**).

Of course, accessories like these do have a learning curve, so you should research all the safety concerns and read all the instructions thoroughly before picking up any BDSM toy. If you're looking for details on the endless supply of instruments for cock-and-ball torture or how to interior decorate your own dungeon, you've got the wrong encyclopedia. But there are several good resources for beginners: GV's *Whipsmart* instructional video, and the books *Sensuous Magic, SM 101, When Someone You Love Is Kinky,* and our favorite title, *Screw the Roses: Send Me the Thorns* (all available online). A.k.a. fetish play. **ErosBoutique.com** has an extensive collection of BDSM gear for both beginners and full-time **gimps**. See also **ExtremeRestraints.com** and **restraints**.

bedroom bling

See **high-end sex toys**.

beginner toys

Are you overwhelmed by the tyranny of choice? Or do the **ball gag** and the **spreader bar** sound a bit too much like Dungeons & Dragons for your taste? A beginner **kit** will be right up your alley. We like BL's Sex Toys 101 Kit (\$\$\$), which comes with the **Nubby G** vibrator, the Silver Bullet **miniature vibrator**, a silicone **Little Flirt** butt plug, and a sampler pack of **lube**. The stylish **Mile-High Kit** is a good place to start, too, with its cool carrying case. If you've got a new backdoor friend, try the **Bend Over Beginner Kit**. Or you can build your own starter kit: Try a **"back" massager** to warm up to the idea of sex toys, a pocket-size **vibrator** that could pass as a flashlight key chain, like BL's Babelight (\$), a **waterproof toy** to play with in the shower, a **G-spot stimulator** to see if that's your (or your partner's) bag, a mini **butt plug** to see if *that's* your (or your partner's) bag, and a **Rabbit Habit**, because it's got a bit of everything.

Once you've figured out what kind of stimulation or penetration gets you off—and we're taking a wild guess that you'll get hooked on at *least* one kind—you can experiment with different toys in that range; nobody expects you to feel comfortable with a full chest **harness** and twelve-inch purple-veined **dildo** plus vibrating butt plug until the second date at the *earliest*. See the index for all the beginner toys featured in the book. See also **communication**.

Ben Wa balls

Traditionally, these are two smooth, solid, occasionally gold-plated, unattached spheres, just a bit bigger than kids' marbles, that a woman inserts into her vagina (keep 'em out of your butt). Sometimes, though, they're two slightly bigger hollow metal balls with a loose weight in each (for more on this version, see **duotone balls**). Apparently, women started using egg-shaped inserts, carved from ivory, centuries ago in Asia—these days, they're round and can be made of steel, plastic, or **Lucite**. Once inserted, the balls are supposed to help tone your **pelvic floor muscles** and, if you're incredibly lucky, lead to sheer ecstasy during your morning commute, say, or while shopping at the grocery

store. Some women prefer to use them in conjunction with a penis or a dildo, like a mini game of pool.

Ben Wa enthusiasts claim that women who don't "get it" have been spoiled by phallic-centric, industrial-strength toys and just haven't learned how to tune into life's more subtle pleasures. (We think it sounds like something Sting's wife would enjoy.) Poo-pooers point out that the balls don't really move around much, no matter how much lube you throw on the situation, because a woman's vagina kind of grabs onto whatever you insert into it. And most vaginas aren't really sensitive enough to get off on stationary objects. So you'd have to jump around, maybe with your hands in the air like you just don't care, in order to feel anything going on down there. And if the balls are heavy, all that jiggling could dislodge them (as could a hefty sneeze, for that matter), at which point you'd be forced to mutter something about losing your marbles before skulking away from

→

your spot in the grocery line. Available at LB or MP ($). For a more effective toy along the same lines, see **Smartballs**.

Bend Over Beginner Kit

This starter **strap-on** kit by **Tantus** comes with two very approachable **silicone** dildos, an adjustable two-strap nylon **harness** that fits hips up to 60 inches in circumference (made of canvas, so it looks wholesome and crunchy, like climbing gear or backpack straps), and a **miniature vibrator** that fits snugly into a pocket located on the front of the harness, meaning she'll get a little clit stimulation while riding you like a bucking bronco and whooping, "Who's your daddy now, bitch?" Warning: The triangular section of the harness that covers the mons is made of purple velvet (which just happens to match the shimmery purple dildos). We know some people can't get enough purple velvet in their lives—we're just

sayin', is all. Available at BL, BF, or GV ($$). See also **anal play**, **Bend Over Boyfriend**, and **kits**.

Bend Over Boyfriend

❶ A must-have for anyone with an anally retentive boyfriend, this instructional video, made by **GoodVibes.com**'s resident sexologist, Carol Queen, and her "partner in life," Robert Morgan Lawrence (they also cofounded the Center for Sex & Culture, in San Fran), teaches hetero couples how to enjoy male penetration with a **strap-on**. The film is occasionally cheesy, but the couples are real, and the **anal play** info is priceless. For years, it was GV's best-selling vid. There's even a *Bend Over Boyfriend 2,* subtly subtitled *More Rockin', Less Talkin'.* And GV (among others) conveniently sells the **Bend Over Beginner Kit**. ❷ A male partner who enjoys taking it up the tookus.

bendable dildos & vibrators

These are the Gumby dolls of the sex-toy world: They come with a flexible spine so you can bend them into whatever pose works for you, because not all **G-spots** are alike (that includes hers *and* his), and not all coochies and tushies are alike, either. Don't contort your body to the toy—make the toy bend to *your* whim! Another upside to the Gumby dildos is that you can use them for **packing** *and* playing. "Is that a bendable dildo in your pocket, or did you just suddenly become even happier to see me?" Most bendy dildos are made of **Cyberskin**, and most bendy vibes are made of **jelly rubber**—both are **porous**, probably have **phthalates**, and should therefore be used with a **condom**. Some popular toys in this genre include the Mr. Bendy Cyberskin dildo (BL; $$$), the Real Deal Softskin dildo (GV; $$), the Technobend Softskin dildo (GV; $$$), the Big Bender vibe (GV; $$), the Bendy-G vibrating dildo (LB; $$), the Flexible Fantasy dildo (MP; $$), and the Flexible Ecstasy water-proof vibe (MP; $$). See also the Rock Your World vibe in the **Rabbit Habit** entry.

Berman Center Intimate Accessories

Dr. Laura Berman, LCSW, PhD, runs Chicago's Berman Center, a specialized health center for women focusing on sexual health and menopause management (BermanCenter.com). She's developed a complete line →

of "hygienically superior and clinically approved" devices that address a wide range of sexual challenges. For the most part, Berman has taken popular toys and tried to improve on them in terms of materials and/or design, so you'll find, for example, a hybrid of the **Hitachi Magic Wand** and the **Wahl vibrator** back massagers that's made *specifically* for the genitals. And a clitoral **pump** called Selene that's based on the one-and-only FDA-approved device for female sexual dysfunction (the Eros CTD). And a clit-slash-**G-spotter** called the Adonis that's more subtly shaped than the **Rock Chick vibrator**. We're not quite sure how the vibrating panties could be improved on from a therapeutic standpoint, but Berman does good work, so we'll go with it.

The insertable toys are 100 percent **silicone**, with the exception of her **pelvic-floor-muscle** toy, Juno (made of **Lucite**), and the noninsertable toys (made of **PVC**). These and more come in unifying shades of purple and pink in elegant packaging with detailed instructions and diagrams about proper use on **EvesGarden.com** ($$-$$$).

Betty's Barbell dildo

Designed by sexologist Betty Dodson, author of the classic masturbation manifesto *Sex for One,* this is a dildo with a strong work ethic: It's built to help you tone your vaginal muscles for improved sexual response and bladder control. Made of super-safe stainless steel (to match all your chi-chi Crate & Barrel kitchen appliances), the Barbell is 6 ¾ inches by 1 ¼ inches and weighs just under a pound (so

B

your **pelvic floor muscles** are pretty much the only ones this baby will work out). Plus, this **metal** barbell can double as a stylish **G-spot toy**. Clean it with soap and water. Available on BL, BF, or GV ($$$). A.k.a. Betty Dodson's Vaginal Barbell. See also **kegels**.

blindfolds

The blindfolds that come free with a transatlantic Virgin flight (oh, really, you shouldn't have, Richard Branson) are printed with the phrase "forty winks"—and we think we know what kind of winks they're talking about. Who *hasn't* stuffed a complimentary blindfold into their carry-on and thought, "Ooh, I should use that sometime"? But, really, you should. You can go **high end** (a suede-and-silk number from JimmyJane.com; $$$) or **DIY** (a cotton scarf or tee knotted to the *side* of the head for comfort).

Blindfolds help you get in the mood if you're trying something new and are feeling shy:

Maybe you want to spank your boyfriend but don't want him to see you until you've perfected your swing; maybe you're role-playing and find it easier to get into character if you can't see that your "doctor" is wearing his stethoscope back to front; etc. And a blindfold is the simplest way to try out **sensation play**: It adds an element of surprise (especially pleasant when receiving cunnilingus) and makes everything feel *more*. You know how your radio always sounds louder after you've turned off your bedside light? Yeah, it's like that, except it's not KROC; it's *sex*! Back in the eighties, people used to say, "It's like sex on acid!" We prefer the more contemporary "It's like sex on broadband!"

Blowfish.com (BF)

Allergic to mission statements, the folks at Blowfish.com rely on the short but sweet tagline "Good products for great sex" to get their message across. And

➜

though they also seem allergic to decent Web design and navigation, their site boasts a big selection of high-quality products at *awesome* prices (consistently the lowest around—as much as $30 cheaper than other outlets in some cases). Around for more than a decade, Blowfish carries only products they think will last, they never use a manufacturer's marketing copy to review products, they take their own photos (which can sometimes look a little low budge), they inspect every glass dildo, they usually pick higher-quality items from small artisans over cheaper versions from mass manufacturers, and they pride themselves on decent customer service (e.g., you'll never get an "Oh, just toggle the power" response).

Blowfish caters to those ready to try something a little bit more adventurous than a **slimline** vibe. (Their video department even has a subsection called "Surrealistic Weird Shit.") And though they sell to *every* persuasion, Blowfish has become the one-stop shopping center for straight guys who want to start experiencing **anal play** for themselves. As BF president Christophe hilariously told us, "No one has ever lost money selling things for straight guys to shove up their butts."

Bodybouncer, the

We don't know if this product— a natural-rubber saddle with a hole in the middle mounted on a steel frame—is the height of ingenuity or the height of laziness. It's intended for hetero couples: The man aligns his erect penis under the hole, and the woman sits on the saddle, which hovers over the man's erection; she then starts to bounce up and down, apparently to ecstasy. This "velvet vise" requires only a slight flexing of the thighs to set it in motion, and very little effort to sustain— the idea being that you won't get tired or cramped or hung up on awkward mechanics.

Of course, it's hard not to imagine horrific "accidents" involving poked cervixes and smashed balls, but the manufacturer claims it's safe: "If you're picturing your intimate anatomy slamming together in precariously imprecise orbits, you're thinking of a sex **swing**, not a Bodybouncer. The Bouncer saddle moves in only one direction—straight up and down—and either partner can control exactly how *much* it travels. Within seconds of setting up, most men realize that they can close their eyes and navigate the experience by feel alone." You can't fully comprehend it until you see it in action, so visit Bodybouncer.com for a video demo. The site's design is slick—and tasteful, to boot! ($$$)

body paint

Who wants to paint the town red when you can stay home and paint each other? Playing with edible finger paints is like having a smokin'-hot Montessori teacher encourage you to "indulge your inner Picasso" while going down on you to help "unleash your creative juices." We bet you ten bucks the first time you try body paint, you won't be able to resist painting cheeky arrows and "open for business" signs. Oh, who are we kidding? We bet you paint cheeky arrows *every* time you try it. The **Kama Sutra** Lover's Paintbox is all chocolate, if that's what you fancy—don't forget a glass of milk for the nightstand. And if James Bond is more your speed, try the Liquid Latex Starter Kit and make like Goldfinger. Liquid Latex dries in minutes, and, unlike paint, it allows the skin to breathe—it's your very own, custom-fitted fetish outfit. The kit comes with red and black **latex** (Catwoman's got nothing on you), plus a few jars of stardust for glamming the whole thing up. Let's see those jazz hands! (All available at BL.)

B

bondage belt

A bad-ass **leather** belt (1¼ inches by 45 inches) that transforms into an easily adjustable figure-eight **restraint** and can be used as a wrist, ankle, or neck restraint. For those times when you suddenly need to drop your pants *and* tie up an errant love slave. Nearly every babe on staff at **Babeland** has bought herself one of these, but for some reason they haven't caught on with the masses (\$\$). See also **BDSM**, **ErosBoutique.com**, and **ExtremeRestraints.com**.

bondage tape

Soft, reusable PVC tape that won't stick to skin, hair, or clothes—only to itself. Good for binding, gagging, even mummifying, but only if you know how! Jay Wiseman's book *SM 101* or Gloria Brame's *Come Hither: A Common Sense Guide to Kinky Sex* are both good places to start. Never cut off circulation or airways, make sure your partner doesn't overheat if you're using a lot of tape, and keep blunt-ended medical scissors nearby for quick release. Usually comes in red or black, 65 feet to a roll; available at BL or GV (\$). See also **BDSM**, **ErosBoutique.com**, **ExtremeRestraints.com**, and **restraints**.

boy toys

It's certainly a sign that times are a'-changin' when a man can walk into a sex-toy shop and ask plaintively, "Where are the toys for me?" (In case you missed it, sex-toy shops weren't exactly female friendly a decade or so back—unless you're using *friendly* as a euphemism for "unwanted leering attention, plus a little indecent exposure if you're lucky.") What the men really mean is, "Where are the toys for my penis?" After all, **butt plugs**, **anal beads**, **strap-on dildos**, and **nipple clamps** are all equal opportunity accessories. Plenty of guys already use their girlfriend's **vibrator** on themselves. And anyone can get tied up with **rope**, spanked with a **flogger**, and called "bitch."

But we know you want toys to call your very own, too, so here are the options for your number-one guy: the **Aneros butt plug**, a cock **ring** (regular or vibrating), **French ticklers**, **masturbation sleeves** (like the **Fleshlight**), and penis **extenders** (worn during sex, either regular or vibrating). You might also want to consider a penis vibrator, like the Hugger Vibrator (BL; $; top illustration below) or the SWAK Kit (GV; $; bottom illustration below), both of which attach to a **miniature vibrator** (included). The Hugger is a tulip-shaped **vinyl** cup—the vibe causes the petals to flutter against the head of his penis—

and the **jelly** SWAK is a sleeve that stretches to fit over the head and then vibrates. Or, you could just buy one of the tulip-shaped attachments that fit onto your girlfriend's **Wahl vibrator** (see **Wahl attachments**). We doubt any of these penis-head vibes will actually get you off (unless you used to masturbate in flower beds as a young boy). Rather, they're a way to tease yourself before a hand job or to let your partner tease you—assuming you're willing to give up the remote, of course. See also **finger toys**, **Fukuoku 9000 finger toy** (Massage Glove), **Laya Spot vibrator**, and **Lelo vibrators**.

Buddy butt plug, the

This massively popular mid-range (3½ inch by 1¼ inch) **butt plug** by **VixenCreations.com** is curved for improved **prostate** stimulation. It doesn't stay in place quite as obediently as other butt plugs, however, and is

→

therefore best suited for gently pulling in and out, rather than leaving in place. For something with a little more staying power, try the **Ryder** plug, by **Tantus**, instead. Buddy is 100 percent silicone, so wash or boil to clean and use with water-based **lube**. Available almost everywhere ($$). See also **anal play**, **butt plugs**, and **P-spot**.

bullet vibrators

Miniature vibrators shaped more like an elongated egg or a symmetrical OB tampon (in its wrapper) than an actual bullet. Not usually intended for insertion, but, rather, for external stim, usually in conjunction with a **miniature-vibrator sleeve** or a cock **ring**. Available everywhere ($).

butt plugs, about

Before you start backing away from this entry, ass cheeks clenched in fear, hear us out: If you've ever enjoyed a little pinky in the bee-hind—or if you've ever even *entertained* the idea of enjoying it some day—you can handle a butt plug. A butt plug is inserted at some point during sex or masturbation and is then pretty much ignored while you go about your business. (Actually, we guess you could insert one before going to pick up the dry cleaning, too—it might make drive-time radio a little more bearable.) All butt plugs have a flared base (so they don't get lost up there), and most are diamond shaped: pointy at the tip for easy entry, wider in the middle, and with a skinny neck just above the base (so they stay in place).

→

Whatever size of butt plug you're working with, the idea is the same: to give you that pleasant "filled-up" feeling, to give your muscles something to clench onto when they contract during orgasm, and to stimulate the **prostate** (if you've got one). Either way, "filled up" is a gender-neutral diversion no matter your sexual orientation—nerve endings are nerve endings, and we've all got plenty back there: The anus contains more nerve endings than any part of the male body, and more than any part of the female body except the clitoris. Plus, for women, getting filled up back there during vaginal penetration can create a knock-on effect, causing the finger or phallus in the front door to stimulate her in brand-new places. See also **Aneros** and **Divine-Interventions.com**.

bigger than that pinkie finger you might have once got jiggy with, except no one's going to get an arm cramp trying to keep it in. (Seriously, if one partner is long bodied and the other is short armed, pinkie action during sex just isn't happening.) Another diminutive option is the Little Zinger, which has a loop in the base, like a pacifier, for easy removal.

butt plugs, beginner

The smallest butt plugs, like the **Little Flirt** (illustrated), are no

butt plugs, intermediate

Once you're ready to graduate from Little League to the minor leagues, consider the über-popular, prostate-friendly

→

Buddy (it's like the Heather of the butt-plug world). For a slight step up (harder to insert but with more staying power once in), try the **Ryder** plug.

butt plugs, large

Are you ready for the big time? You might never be, but, just in case, we've got four words for you: **Tristan 2 butt plug**. Oh, wait, we've got three more for you: Lots. Of. **Lube**.

butt plugs with a twist

Less-traditional, knobbly butt plugs like the silicone **Ripple butt plug** are meant more for pulling in and out than leaving be. Or, if you're finding your butt plug a little lifeless and dull, consider upgrading to a vibrating plug, like the silicone **Pro-Touch** or Vibratex's **elastomer** Tushy plug, which feels like **Cyberskin** but is actually **latex** free and **phthalate** free (BF, on BL as the Tulip; $$). **Vibratex** also has a similar plug called the Stopper, made from food-grade **vinyl**, but it's harder to find in stores. Sensitive tushes might prefer the soft feel of the squishier rubber toys to the harder silicone of most plugs, but those are **porous** and thus harder to keep clean (especially if you're not using a condom!). Or perhaps what you're missing in your plug is more of a *je ne sais quoi?* Role-players, **BDSM** dabblers, or animal lovers might enjoy plugs with horsetails or feather plumes attached (illustrated; EB, EX, BL; $$). And you thought *your* Halloween costume went the extra mile. See also **riding crops**.

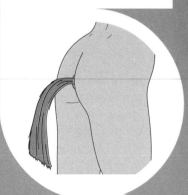

butt toys

See **anal play**.

Butterfly Effect wearable vibrator

Pop-quiz time, kids! The Butterfly Effect is ❶ a long-forgotten movie starring Ashton Kutcher, ❷ a widely misappropriated aspect of chaos theory, or ❸ a wearable, *waterproof* **triple-action vibrator**? We'll take door number three, Monty! This ten-speed vibe is a solo toy, unlike the **butterfly vibrators with harnesses**, which encourage company. The head of this butterfly buzzes the **clitoris**, the body acts as a dildo to stimulate a woman's **G-spot**, and the tail (do butterflies even *have* tails?) tickles the surface of the anus—all kept in place by adjustable straps worn around the hips and thighs.

The Butterfly Effect is too bulky to wear in public (again, unlike the butterfly vibes with harnesses), but it makes great company in a bath (just make sure the battery compartment is closed and dry inside) or while "cybering." Try it during phone sex if chat rooms aren't your thing—or, hell, wear it next time you watch a dirty movie, and you can get some crocheting done at the same time! The butterfly part is porous **jelly**, but its design makes using a condom with it damn near impossible, so make sure you at least keep it **monogamous**. Wash with mild soap and water. Watch batteries included (GV; $$). Non-waterproof versions with AA battery packs include the Mutant Butterfly (BF) and Buzzing Butterfly (MP).

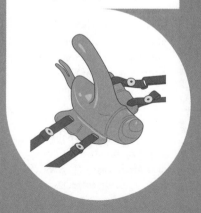

butterfly vibrators with harnesses

Back when we were little girls daydreaming about growing up to become sex-advice columnists for a living, we used to imagine that one day, something like this pretty butterfly would flutter down to save us all from nonorgasmic penetrative sex. It comes in a few versions, but the basic gist is the same: A **miniature vibrator** sits snugly inside a **jelly** butterfly-shaped sleeve, which sits on a woman's clitoris and is held in place by a harness. The vibrations cause the wings to flutter over the clitoris, and the whole contraption is so small that you can have sex any way you wish without it getting in the way. Which means—*hello!*—vibrating clitoral stimulation during intercourse! (Just like with a vibrating cock **ring**, except the vibe is worn by her instead of by the penetrator.)

Of course, there's no particular reason the jelly sleeve should be shaped like a butterfly—it just happens that most of them are. There's the nerd-chic **Audi-Oh butterfly vibrator** ($$$), of course, or LB's Flutter Bug ($$) and MP's Gossamer Butterfly ($$$, because it's cordless), which both come with variable speeds and a jock-strap-style harness (allowing for easy penetration; see **harnesses**). WT went all out with their Leather Butterfly ($$), which does the same thing, but is made of—you guessed it—black **leather**.

Then there's the Remote Butterfly (illustrated on page 42; available almost everywhere; $$$), which comes with a wireless **remote control** with a 25-foot range. This one has an elastic G-string-style harness you have to kind of push aside to make way for penetration—thus, this toy is better suited for nonpenetrative play or masturbation, either at home or in public. The butterfly will fit easily under your clothes, assuming you're not into Lycra. Warning: If you're out and about, just be sure to use it in a crowded bar or loud club—its vibes are a bit too noisy for

B

→

that quiet romantic candlelit dinner.

If you've got something against butterflies (we bet you hate rainbows and ponies, too), check out the heart-shaped Sweetheart vibrator (BL, and MP calls it the Heart Throb; $$). Same vibrating deal, though not exactly an improvement in terms of corniness.

Jelly toys should be monogamous and can be washed in soap and water. Because of the **phthalates** in jelly, you can use a **dental dam** as a barrier between your skin and the toy—especially recommended if the toy is really cheap or rubbery smelling, or if you're planning on wearing it all evening long. See also **Butterfly Effect wearable vibrator**.

C

California Exotics Novelties

The California Exotics Novelties company (calexotics.com) takes a very macho approach to toy sales: quantity over quality. But we gotta hand it to them: They distribute about a *bazillion* toys. And they're the go-to co. for celebrities wanting a branded line of toys with limitless distribution (see **Berman Center Intimate Accessories** and **Sue Johanson's Royal Line**). Plus, they have a line of **phthalate**-free products—with "phthalate free" actually advertised on the packaging (made for European clients whose uppity governments demand product safety). Most of their generic toys are made from crappy **plastic** or **jelly** and come in packaging even Britney Spears would find distasteful.

candles

Some things should never be attempted in fluorescent overhead lighting: first dates, marriage proposals, and rimming, to name just a few. Everything looks better in candlelight—so why should the goths have all the fun? But beware: That two-dollar Hindu-goddess candle you bought at Urban Outfitters is for decorative purposes only. If you're going to actually drip wax onto your luvver, you need to buy the right kind of candle (see **candle wax**).

candle wax

Here's a quick science lesson for you: Scented and colored **candles** often contain plasticizers, which make them burn much hotter—i.e., way too hot for your sweetie's fleshy parts. Black candles and beeswax candles burn the hottest of all. (Besides, black candles are so Trenchcoat Brigade.) You're better off with the plain white paraffin candles sold at grocery and hardware stores for "emergencies" (and don't even think about filching the candles from your terrorism-survival backpack). Better still are soy candles, which burn cleaner and at an even lower temperature than paraffin.

The stop, drop, and rolls of hot-wax play: Blow the candle out before dripping the wax; test the wax on the back of your hand first; once the wax hits their skin, rub it in to disperse the heat; do not drip the wax on your partner's face; and, finally, do not indulge in candle play on your brand-new Tempur-Pedic bed with your $500 Calvin Klein sheet set. In fact, to avoid picking dried wax out of carpets and back hair, go for a purpose-made **massage** candle—its wax melts into a body oil when rubbed, without any messy buildup. Try BL's Body Wax Candles ($), GV's Massage Candles ($), or Sunset Mountain's Lava Lotions (BF; $), all of which come in various scents like vanilla, lavender, mango, cucumber, and sandalwood (or just unscented). Alternate with **ice** for extreme **sensation play**.

canes

Long, stiff sticks made for whacking (bottoms mostly). This prop goes nicely with a school-marm outfit, complete with cat-eye glasses and a tight, white, buttoned-down shirt. (Decades ago, teachers really did use canes on trouble makers for corporal rather than erotic punishment.) But a cane is no joke: It can cause severe bruising and welts, especially when you don't know where and how to wield it. Unlike a **paddle** or a good hand spank, a cane causes sharp and stinging pain. The tip travels faster than the hand wielding it, so use the lower part of the cane for a less intense blow. Fortunately, canes, unlike **whips**, are easy to handle at slower speeds. So definitely go slow! See **BDSM** for more on safety resources. See also **floggers** and **riding crops**.

chaps

Assless, crotchless, **leather** pants meant to be worn over jeans for motorcycle riding. For obvious reasons, they were adopted by the gay leather community, which grew out of the sixties counterculture. If the word *chaps* came up during a word-association game, Tom of Finland or the Village People would probably spring to mind.

chopsticks

Asian utensils, which can be used to eat sushi off your luvver (wasabi belongs on the nips, far away from the nether regions; soy sauce can go in the belly button), or to fashion your own homemade **nipple clamps** (bind two chopsticks together by wrapping a rubber band around each end).

cleaning & care

Any toy you buy *should* come with specific cleaning instructions—if it doesn't (and no "**novelties**" do), be sure to ask or e-mail one of the nice sex-toy salespeople for advice (and if there are no nice sex-toy salespeople in sight, shame on you for not shopping at one of our recommended outlets). Do we have to say, Follow these instructions? Yes, we think we do: *Follow these instructions.* Dirty sex toys can spread disease and cause infection, so wash them before their first use, immediately after every use (as opposed to just waiting to clean it before the next time), and immediately before each use, too, if you're not **storing** it correctly (i.e., if it's gathering dust bunnies under your bed). To prevent corrosion of motor parts and battery compartments, don't immerse vibrators in water unless they're waterproof (and even then, make sure the battery pack is sealed tightly). Instead, use a washcloth to carefully soap it up and rinse it. Whatever the product, allow it to thoroughly air dry before storing it away.

The *only* sex toys you should be sharing without a condom are those that are **non-porous**. **Silicone** toys (without built-in vibrators) are best, because they can be sterilized in boiling water for several minutes. (If it has a removable vibrator, be sure to remove it first.) But if, like one of the authors of this book, you are particularly forgetful and could imagine leaving a silicone dildo in boiling water on the stove top while running out to the gym and returning an hour later to a postnuclear mass of melted silicone welded to your pan, you might want to just pop it on the top shelf of your dishwasher to disinfect it (again, sans any plastic or vibe parts).

Don't use any harsh dishwashing detergents if you're using the dishwasher—with all the heat and water, you shouldn't need it. If the dildo is a **monogamous** dildo, you can just wash it off with antibacterial soap and water. If you like to share, boiling is best. Hard

➜

C

acrylic (a.k.a. Lucite), **glass**, and **metal** toys should not be boiled, though they can be shared without condoms if you clean them really thoroughly (with antibacterial soap and hot water), as they are non-porous. Toys made of all other materials—**Cyberskin**, soft **elastomer**, **jelly rubber**, **latex**, soft **vinyl**—should be cleaned with soap and water and must *not* be shared without a condom, as they are **porous**.

In fact, though we fully understand the desire to ride one's dildo bareback, if you use a condom with these **materials**, not only will cleanup be a cinch, but your self-love will be **safer** (especially if you're using a toy that might be seeping **phthalates**). Keep in mind, however, that cheap toys are often so poorly designed that they can't be cleaned properly. For instance, if a toy has seams but can't be taken apart without it breaking, it'll never get *really* clean; those nooks and crannies can harbor bacteria that's harmful to sensitive **vaginal** and anal canals. Finally,

most sex-toy stores sell bottled sex-toy cleaners; while purpose-made cleaners like these might make you feel more secure about passing the white-glove test, they're no better than a good scrub with soap and water.

Clitoral Hummer waterproof vibrator

———

We have to hand it to **California Exotics Novelties**: This shimmery silver vibe actually works. The head of this hard **plastic** toy looks like a little hooded elf in profile, and the body is gently curved, so it feels pretty good to hold. That said, because the entire thing—as opposed to just the head—vibrates, your hand and arm will start to feel all jangly pretty quickly, especially on the highest setting, which is very strong.

Though this low-pitched vibrator *can* be used internally (the little nubbin on the tip of

➜

C

the elf's hood can stimulate the **G-spot**–or any particular spot, for that matter), the really neato part is the scooped-out section that can cup the **clitoris**. Imagine holding a shallow, vibrating ice cream scooper over your **clitoris**, and you get the idea. It's great for particularly sensitive clits, because the **vibrator** doesn't actually touch down on the clitoral head (unless you've got a slightly larger-than-average clit); it just cradles it from above and disperses vibrations throughout the genital area. If you decide you want to switch to more direct clit stimulation, you can just flip it over–bam! All that, and you can take it in the bath, too. We'd say $ (at BF) is a friggin' bargain–though, admittedly, it's pretty cheap looking. The Clitoral Hummer goes by various aliases elsewhere: the Hummingbird at BL, the Contoured Pearl at MP, and the Leia at WT. Wash in antibacterial soap and water (make sure the two-AA battery-compartment hatch is screwed on *really* tight

before submerging). See also **bath accessories**, **clitoris**, and **waterproof toys**.

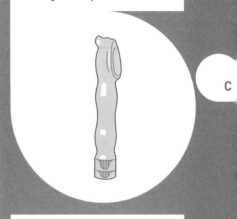

C

clitoris

The clitoris is the only organ in the human body (either male or female) whose sole purpose is to transmit sexual sensation. And it goes much deeper than you'd think (kind of like a Barbara Walters special): It's actually a complex organ that extends *throughout* a woman's genitals and is therefore sometimes referred to as the clitoral network. To keep things simple, however, whenever we use the words *clit* or *clitoris* in this book, we're referring just to the clitoral glans, or head—that sensitive little nubbin you all know and love as the clitoris. For those of you on the short bus: The nubbin sits in a little hood where the tops of the labia meet. It's analogous to the glans of the penis.

Most women need some kind of clitoral stimulation in order to come—and who can blame them? The clitoral head has more sensory nerve endings than any other structure in the body (again, female *or* male)—somewhere between 6,000 and 8,000, four times as many as on the (much larger) head of the penis. And, just like the penis, the clitoris fills with blood and swells when it's aroused. But not all clitorises are alike, as you should know if you've had the pleasure of knowing more than one in your life. Some are smaller than a grain of rice, and others are the size of a lima bean (talk about flicking the bean). Some are very shy and rarely peek out of the hood, and others are big show-offs. Some disappear into

the hood once they're aroused, and others pop out when they're turned on. Some women like direct clitoral stimulation, and others prefer it over the hood—and some find even *that* too intense. And clitorises have mood swings, too—what's too much on Monday may feel just right on Wednesday. It's a matter of experimenting—on yourself or your partner—until you find what works.

The toys listed at the end of this entry are a great place to start. Remember that most clits can take more (and more varied) stimulation when you use **lube** and/or when the woman is very turned on. Start on the lowest setting with any toy and work your way up so you don't give the poor clit a heart attack. And if the clitoris in question isn't yours, pay constant attention to the woman upstairs—you need the feedback. Want to read more? We know of no better resource than *The Clitoral Truth*, by our friend Rebecca Chalker. It's a must-read for anyone with a vagina in their life. A.k.a. chickpea, little man in the boat, magic button, nubbin. See also **butterfly vibrators with harnesses**, **Clitoral Hummer waterproof vibrator**, clitoral **pumps**, vibrating cock **rings**, **sensitizing creams**, and **vibrators**.

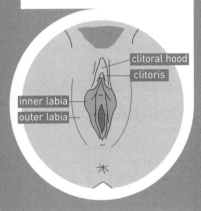

clothespins

DIY approach to **nipple clamps** for advanced players only (due to their being nonadjustable). Word to the wise: Brand-new clothespins will grip way harder than the ones your grandmother has been using to hang out her laundry for the past sixty years. Hey, what Grandma doesn't know won't perv her out. If

you're looking for something to match your dungeon, try BL's Hot Grip clothespins—they're black with rubber tips; $ for a pack of twenty-five.

cock rings

See **rings, cock or penis**.

collars

Classic **BDSM** accoutrements worn by submissives as a symbol of their status. Go with purpose-made ones for humans rather than **DIY** pet collars. **Blowfish** has a wide variety of mostly **leather** collars with silver studs, metal spikes, rings for leash or **restraint** attachments, and different linings for added comfort (or discomfort, as the case may be). They vary in width from a slim ¾ inch for a simple Victorian-choker-necklace look to a thick chin-to-clavicle brace for forced posture. Allow room for at least two fingers between skin and collar, lead around from the front (never tug on the back), and don't ever hang anyone up by one—duh. ($–$$$ at BF, EB, EX.)

ComeAsYou Are.com

"We don't care if you're liberal or conservative, queer or straight, a religious Mormon or the Anti-Christ—we all have the right to sexual exploration, and we all deserve to have a place to go to talk about it without baggage or judgment." So say the folks at Come As You Are, probably the best sex-toy outfitter north of the border (with a retail shop in Toronto). It is one of only two co-op sex stores in the world, the first being **Good Vibes**. In fact, the company was able to open its doors thanks to the financial support of Joani Blank, GV's founder.

Come As You Are also specializes in providing accessible services to people living with physical and developmental disabilities. One of their worker-owners, Cory Silverberg, coauthored *The Ultimate Guide to Sex and Disability*. He's also had the honor of being **Sue Johanson**'s sex-toy wrangler for the past six years. "The only drag about our name," Cory explained to us, "is that when you do a Google search, the other things that come up are Nirvana, of course, and a lot of church Web sites—apparently the 'Come as you are' motto is big with the churches."

communication

Or, how to introduce sex toys to your J.Crew-clad partner, who thinks **vibrators** are for "tattooed weirdos and lezzies." The first step in getting your partner to give sex toys a chance is to figure out what it is he or she has against orgasms. Okay, so maybe you shouldn't put it quite so antagonistically, but you *do* need to determine the exact breed of the bug up their ass, by asking *gently*, outside of the bedroom.

Does he think it's "too tacky," "too desperate," or "too soon" in the relationship to go down that road? Reassure him

→ that a) You'll start with the basics: something small, discreet, and quiet—he'll barely notice it's there! b) you're not going to run out of new toys to try—exhibit A, this book! and c) you don't think it's too soon to have an orgasm, and, frankly, you could use the help. Of course, that last point has to be approached with the utmost delicacy.

Remember, when it comes to sex, his ego is more sensitive than an orphaned baby duckling. Remind him, "It's not you; it's my mechanics." Adding a toy is about your body, not his shortcomings. Suggest something small (to ward off **dildo envy**), quiet (so he can't blame the toy for killing the mood), and preferably non-penis shaped (remember the duckling?). And hand over the toy or battery-pack control to him, explaining that it's way hotter when *he's* wielding your **Pocket Rocket**. If he's concerned about your toy's sexual history, take him shopping and ask him to pick out something new for you. Maybe you can break him in with a vibrating cock **ring** or a **jelly-rubber** cock ring with a nubbin—that way, he's still driving, and you still (might) get off. Whatever you do, don't let him shame you into forgoing your favorite toy forever—a person has to have some limits.

If, on the other hand, you're a toy whore and *she* insists she's not "that kind of girl," remind her of that *Sex and the City* episode where über-prude Charlotte spends some quality time with her **Rabbit Habit**. Or take her to a Web site like **Babeland.com** or **GoodVibes.com** (or, even better, to one of their in-person stores if you happen to be in N.Y.C., Seattle, San Fran, Boston, or L.A.) so she can witness firsthand that you don't have to be "that kind of girl" to shop there. Check out **beginner toys** for a list of suggested implements that would barely shock your grandmother. Whatever you choose, if it's going to be a surprise present and its packaging isn't up to Martha Stewart standards, then remove the toy and put it in a nice gift box. See also **etiquette, gift giving** and **etiquette, recycling**.

C

condoms

Great for keeping your toys **clean**, bacteria free, and STD free. Plus, when you slap one on your dildo, it'll never complain that the sex feels "like clapping with gloves on"! Invest in some decent water-based or silicone-based **lube** and a high-quality, sensation-enhancing condom like Pleasure Plus or Kimono Micro Thins to maximize pleasure. Use only water-based or silicone-based **lubricants** with **latex** condoms or latex **dental dams**, because oil of any kind—Vaseline and hand lotion included—destroys latex. Also, steer clear of so-called water-*soluble* lubes, which frequently contain oil, and take a pass on rubbers with the spermicide **Nonoxynol-9**. Try the Pleasure Condom Sampler from Condomania.com ($) to see which pole sock you like best.

Always use them on toys employed by more than one person or on toys that go from anus to vadge (or any other orifice for that matter), swapping the condom out between holes. If it's a **monogamous** toy, you won't need to use a condom with it so long as all the following criteria are met: You clean the toy thoroughly (between uses *and* orifices), you **store** it properly, and it's made of a high-quality **material** that doesn't contain **phthalates**, porous or not (though the less **porous**, the better).

If you're the MacGyver type, use condoms to turn a **miniature vibrator** into an insertable toy—just be extra careful to keep a hold of the end of the condom on the outside of your bod!

Keep condoms in a cool, dry place (not your wallet), never reuse them, and chuck 'em on the expiration date. If you're allergic to latex, try polyurethane condoms instead (which are compatible with water-based, and silicone-based, *and* oil-based lubes, by the way). See also the Safety Tips Appendix.

contour toys

Did you hear the one about the girl who got carpal tunnel from her dime-store vibrator? Ergonomic design and sex toys are not two concepts you hear discussed in the same sentence very often, but some forward-thinking designers are starting to catch on. Hey, if we can have ergonomic toothbrushes and razors, why not ergo **vibrators**? Enter contour toys. They're designed to fit comfortably around a woman's curves, they're easy to hold and control, and they look more like bathroom accessories than sex toys (which you may appreciate when going through airport security). Most importantly, they're designed by people who know from vaginas. They're the polar opposite of **novelties**, basically. The two biggest names in contour toys right now are **Emotional Bliss** and **Natural Contours**. Other contour toys include the **Laya Spot vibrator**, the **Lelo vibrators**, the **Pure Bliss vibrator**, and the **Rock Chick vibrator**.

Cosmic vibrator

It's not just a party in your pants with the deep-purple, glittery, 7½-inch Cosmic **G-spotter** vibe; it's a disco inferno! This toy has the classic come-hither curve, with a rounded knob on the tip that vibrates gently and steadily for direct **G-spot** action. The wider shaft vibrates with more vigor to stimulate the outer third of the **vagina**, where all the nerve endings are. Just add two AA batteries for a boogie night. It's made of **jelly rubber**, so wash with soap and water, and *always* use with a condom (\$ at BL).

C

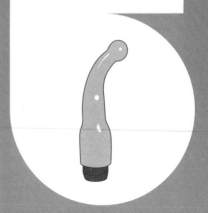

crotchless underwear

❶ Just what it sounds like.
❷ An oxymoron.

cuffs

Sometimes it's nice to have an excuse to lie back and receive pleasure without lifting a finger. And **restraints** for wrists and ankles (sometimes even for thumbs) give you just that. Purpose-made cuffs are certainly safer and more comfortable than metal police-style ones (which can cause nerve damage), and they're quicker to put on

and take off than complicated nylon-**rope** bondage. Available in nylon, silk, **leather**, fur, and faux fur (or some combination thereof) with Velcro clasps, buckles, or locks (make sure they're adjustable to get the right fit). Often, they'll come with tethers a few feet long (to tie to bedposts, for example), rings to which you can attach your own tethers, or clasps that you can simply attach to each other.

Start with the cleverly named Jane's Bonds—two nylon cuffs with faux-fur lining and 4-foot tethers (\$\$ at LB, WT, BL). Or, get more bang for your buck with the Prisoner of Love Kit, which comes with basic wrist and ankle cuffs (four in all), each with tethers, plus a **blindfold**, all for \$\$ (LB, GV). If you don't have anything near the bed to tie the tethers to, try Under the Bed Restraints (\$\$ on EX and BL). You position the four straps (adjustable for different-size beds) under the mattress wherever you choose and attach the adjustable cuffs wherever you'd like your loved one's appendages pinned down.

➜

→

When you're done, simply remove the cuffs and tuck away the straps until next time. Finally, for standing-up restraint without having to take a Home Depot workshop on dungeon-hardware installation, try Door Jam Cuffs ($ at BF; $$ at BL or GV). See also **BDSM**, **bondage belt**, and **bondage tape**.

Cyberskin et al.

Cyberskin, manufactured by **novelties** giant Topco, is the most well-known brand of artificial sex-toy material—it feels *so* flesh-like, it's a little creepy. Other brands include Cyber Jel-lee, Eroskin, Futurotic, Softskin, Ultraskin, and UR3—though retailers often use these terms interchangeably (and therefore inaccurately) to mean super-soft material that feels like skin. Used mostly for **masturbation sleeves**, **dildos**, and **softpacks** that are meant to hold a mirror up to life.

Unfortunately, these holes and poles are very **porous**, which means they can't be sterilized and can transmit bacteria and **STDs**,

even after a good cleaning. The base materials are usually combinations of **silicone** and **latex**; the more latex in a "skin" product, the more it seeps oils (eww!). But they may also be made from unstable vinyl (PVC), as Futurotic is, so that means they may contain **phthalates**, which have been connected with health probs. And because the names are all used interchangeably, you can never be sure that the product you're looking at *doesn't* contain phthalates. Thus, you should probably use a **condom** (hey, just like in real life!) to keep things safer and make cleanup a breeze.

After use, **clean** your skin-like product with mild soap and water, *completely* air dry it *inside and out,* and dust with cornstarch (*not* cervical cancer-causing talcum powder) to help stave off the inevitable: the material getting sticky, discolored, and generally nasty. **Store** in a cool, dry place away from intense light sources, like, um, the sun.

Handle carefully, because this kind of material tears easily. Don't use oil-based **lubes** (which will react with the latex,

→

C

if there's any in the toy), and don't use silicone lube (which will react with the silicone, if any), unless of course you *want* your fake-flesh dong to melt like a flesh-colored ice cream cone. And you're going to need a lot of lube (water-based only), because the pores soak it up (ironically, the lube will also make it degrade faster).

A better option is a toy made from Vibratex's fleshlike but phthalate-free **elastomer** they call Softwear, like their vibrating Tushy **butt plug** or their elastomer vibes mentioned in the **Rabbit Habit & Rabbit Pearl vibrators** entry. The *best* alternative, though, is **VixSkin**, from VC—a lifelike material made of **nonporous silicone** that you can sterilize by boiling! (And the name VixSkin is *not* used interchangeably with the others, so you can be sure it's safe, too.) **Tantus Silicone** should have its own safe version out by now—it was too late for us to test drive for this book, but knowing Tantus, we have no doubt it will be equally miraculous. Yay, silicone!

D

dental dams

To the two people who actually paused to read this entry: Yay for you! We bet you never wore a hipster trucker hat, either. It's not easy being a dental-dam girl or guy—popular wisdom has it that "no one" uses them, after all. It's true: The majority of people are pretty lackadaisical when it comes to dams. They know that oral is safer than intercourse, so they just don't bother. But that shouldn't be good enough for you, damn it.

Using a dental dam during cunnilingus or analingus (a.k.a. rimming) can help prevent the transmission of **STDs** like herpes, gonorrhea, chlamydia, syphilis, and HIV (both ways). A dental dam—sometimes referred to as an oral-sex dam—is basically just a square of **latex** laid flat over the vulva or tushy in question. A piece of sturdy **Saran Wrap** will do fine, as will a cut-open, unlubricated condom or

→

latex glove (wash any powder off the latter first, as talc has been linked to cervical cancer).

But if you're going to buck the trend and go damming, why not treat yourself to a custom-made product? Sheer Glyde **Latex** Dams (BL, LB, WT, BF; about $1 each) are built for licking, which means they're designed to transmit sensation, they're flavored, and they're FDA approved for STD protection during oral sex and even rimming! (Who knew the FDA was allowed to discuss rimming?) GV's own Slicks Dams (about $1.50 each) are sold in condom-size packages to fit in your wallet—perhaps the packaging will help dams overcome their stigma, too. Or check out a polyurethane version called Hot Dam (GV, WT; about $1 each)—flavorless, odorless, great if you've got latex allergies, and better than latex at transmitting heat and sensation, too! (Plus, no latex aftertaste.) If you can't keep your dam in place, take a tip from the ladies at **A-Womans-Touch.com** and attach it with a garter belt. Whatever kind you choose, a wee drop of the right kind of lube *under* the dam will make things feel much nicer for all parties involved.

desensitizing creams, anal

After a tough day in the sex-writing biz, we have been known to refer to anal desensitizing creams as the roofies of the lube world, but that's probably a bit harsh. Nevertheless, they are seriously bad-news **lubes**. They numb your chocolate starfish so that **anal play** doesn't hurt so bad. But here's the thing: If it hurts, it means you're not relaxed enough, you're not using enough lube, or you're just plain not doing it right. So your pain receptors are a good thing, geddit? They're like a "Keep Out" sign for your asshole. Sure, creams like Anal-Eze (from über-cheesy, occasionally sleazy sex-toy distributor **California Exotics Novelties**) might let someone plow right through that roadblock, but we like to think that listening to your body is just part of good sex. Besides, Anal-Eze is petroleum based, which means it's not compatible with latex condoms. Unprotected anal sex? Now, there's an even worse idea. If you need yet more convincing, responsible sex-toy shops like **Babeland** and **GoodVibes** don't even stock desensitizing creams. And you know who *does* give a thumbs-up to anal desensitizers? **Porn stars** who specialize in anal sex, that's who. So, you know, if you want to just *pretend* like you're enjoying the anal, go ahead and desensitize, but don't come crying to us when you end up in the emergency room.

desensitizing creams, penis

If a lube or cream claims to give a man "staying power," it's a desensitizer. It probably has a cheeky name, too, like Man-Delay. Call us crazy, but isn't the whole point of sex to *feel* something? Who wants to numb their freakin' *penis*? And not only that, but the cream is bound to rub off on your partner.

Just try explaining to your girlfriend why she suddenly can't feel her vagina. And then get ready to apologize real good, because it's kinda hard to come when you've got a numb veegee. Besides, it's not like these creams have even been proven to work—not even the "ancient Chinese penis balm," we're afraid—so why take the risk? If you really want to go longer, try a cock **ring** instead. If you've got a serious premature-ejaculation problem, there are safer, nontopical treatments: training your body during masturbation practice, seeing a sex therapist, or wearing **extenders** or even just thick Trojan condoms. See also **lubes**; **sensitizing creams**; and **tightening creams, vaginal**.

dildo envy

❶ The coveting of your best friend's titanium **Elemental Pleasures** vibrator set she got at her bachelorette party.
❷ The wish that your own dick was as long, thick, veiny, and/or vibratory as your partner's favorite **dildo**.

D

dildos, about

❶ Phallic-shaped objects that can be worn or held and used to do things that penises are famous for, like penetrating a vagina, an asshole, or even a mouth (see **strap-on blow jobs**), or just filling out a nice pair of Levi's (see **softpacks**). A dildo doesn't vibrate or move unless *you* move it. The only exception is a vibrating dildo (see page 65). Most dildos have a flared base so they can be worn in **harnesses** or inserted into the butt without fear of getting lost up there. If a dildo *doesn't* have a flared base—like many **glass** dildos, for example—that means it's a handheld dildo and should not be used in the butt. If you don't like harnesses but still want to wear your dildo, see **dildos, double**. Any dildo meant for using—as opposed to wearing in your underpants—will be erect; only **softpacks** are flaccid. If you plan to hold the dildo in your hand, any kind will work. If you intend to employ your dildo solo, try one with a suction-cup base like the Master Suction

Cup Dildo (BF; $$) or the Big Red (BL; $$): Just stick it to the shower wall, bend over to pick up your bar of soap, and—oooh, *hello,* sailor!

Many people think of dildos as a stand-in for a penis; others think those narrow-minded people should go fuck themselves. Increasingly, dildos *don't* resemble dismembered penises. Aside from the fact that a pale-apricot penis with bulging blue veins just isn't as pretty as some of the glittery options out there, many women feel that a "realistically veined" (that's a technical term, we swear) dildo sends the message that a woman needs a man—or, more specifically, his penis—to get off. It's kind of like soy "meat" products: Some **vegetarians** like their tofu prodded and molded until it resembles a hot dog or even a full-grown turkey, while others think this sends the message that **vegans** are just repressed carnivores (tofucking, anyone?). See also **dildos, non-realistic** and **dildos, realistic**.

Dildos aren't just for lesbians, by the way. A straight

D

woman can buttfuck her boyfriend (or even–*gasp*–her husband!) with a dildo. A straight or gay man can use a dildo as a kind of wingman, while his own penis and hands are busy with other orifices or body parts, or after his own penis has exhausted itself. And anyone can use a dildo during masturbation–some people like something to grip onto or something poking their **G-spot** while they get to their happy place.

❷ A tiny (population 1,200) town in Newfoundland, Canada. This hamlet has been called Dildo for centuries. Some people claim the town was named after the sex toys Nordic women used to carve from whalebone, but, then again, some people are still forwarding the Neiman-Marcus cookie recipe, too. Back in the eighties, a few residents of Dildo proposed changing the town's name, but in a vote, tradition won out, and you can still find Dildo on the map. Which we think is kind of sweet. See also **dildos, history of**.

See the Toy Guide for a listing of dildos in this book.

dildos, double

Double **dildos** are designed to give the penetrator a little (or more than a little) penetrat*ing.* They work like this: One end goes in a person's vagina (if they have one) or ass, and the other end goes in their partner's vagina (if they have one) or ass. Kind of like the spaghetti scene in *Lady and the Tramp,* except with a dildo, and orifices other than mouths. The original versions you see in tacky sex shops are straight and look like a British bobby's police truncheon; with those, you'd have to employ some tricky positions and maneuvers. Much better, at least for women penetrating their girlfriends or boyfriends, are those built on an angle– somewhere between 45 and 90 degrees. She grips on with her vagina for dear life–*hello,* **kegels**!–and then thrusts. (The driver *can* be male and can drive with his bumhole–if, say, his dick is out of commission or his partner wants to try a different size for a change–but this is much less common.)

→

D

If you tend to be a little lazy about doing your kegels, nothing inspires like a double dildo! Try practicing solo–insert your end of the DD and watch the other end bounce up and down as you contract your **pelvic floor muscles**. In fact, if you're home alone with your double dildo and none of the other kids will play with you, you can even use the dildo to target your **G-spot** or **P-spot**: Insert it as usual and use the "poking" end as a handle.

In addition to providing double penetration, DDs also do away with the need for a **harness**, which can make the whole dildo-diddling process feel smoother and more natural. That said, even a double dildo will feel more sturdy when strapped into a harness–it all depends on how much work your pelvic floor muscles are willing to do. A pair of button-fly jeans or well-fitting tighty-whities can provide a similar support structure–plus, that's kind of hot. The most popular DDs out there are the **Feeldoe** by **Tantus**, and the **Nexus** by **Vixen Creations**.

dildos, ejaculating

We know what some of you are thinking: What kind of **dildo** party is it if nobody comes? *All right,* if you insist: The Peter North Ejaculating Cock (BL; $$$) is the ultimate in **realistic dildos**: It's molded after **porn star** Peter North, and it vibrates (okay, so maybe not *that* realistic). You can fill it with warm water and squeeze the balls to make it–you guessed it–"ejaculate" at the appropriate time. It's made of a jelly-vinyl combo, so definitely use a condom if it's going anywhere inside. As **Babeland.com** recommends, you can pull out and rip off the condom for the "money shot."

dildos, history of

It's not *impossible* that a town in Canada–see **dildos, about**, second definition–was named after a faux phallus. After all, the dirty meaning of the word *dildo* has been in English usage since at least the seventeenth century (in 1673, the Earl of Rochester penned a rather indelicate ballad called "Signor Dildo"), and dildos themselves have been around since at least 10,000 BC (just ask the archaeologists). The ancient Chinese made theirs out of jade and bronze, and the ancient Greeks used **leather**, wood, or stone (olive oil was their **DIY lube** of choice back then). In Renaissance Italy they called their silver or ivory phalluses *dilettos,* and in Victorian England they called the rubber dong "the widow's comforter."

dildos, materials for

These days, most dildos are made of **silicone**, and most of the high-quality silicone dildos on the market are manufactured by either **Tantus** or **Vixen Creations**, though stores often sell them under different names, so it's hard to tell. (Hint: Though Tantus doesn't sell directly to consumers, VC does on its Web site, and the prices are significantly lower than if you go via a retailer.) Pure silicone makes for a great dildo, because it's easy to clean, it retains body heat (so as not to feel like a speculum in there), it's durable, it doesn't get sticky or tacky, it's **phthalate** free, and it's nice and firm, while still having a bit of give.

Then there are the more fleshlike **Cyberskin** dildos, though, being made of unstable, **porous** material, their shelf life is pretty brief (as opposed to a silicone dildo, which can last for years, if not a lifetime). Unfortunately, Cyberskin and its ilk (Softskin, etc.) may give off **phthalates**, plus they're super absorbent, which means you have to use a ton of **lube**. We've even heard of a Cyberskin dildo getting, er, stuck back there, because all the lube got absorbed. The moral of the story? Whack on a condom. **Jelly** dildos are way cheaper than silicone or Cyberskin, though price is pretty much the only thing they have going for them. They get very tacky, they're hard to clean, they smell like jelly, they degrade easily, they contain phthalates, and they're kinda wobbly (who wants a wobbly dick?).

However, a cheap 'n' cheerful (less than twenty bucks) rubber-jelly dildo like BL's Ballsy Supercock or LB's Randy, dressed up in a condom, isn't a bad way to figure out what size is right for you before you go splashing out on a silicone dong. Of course, you could just as easily perform this experiment with a selection from the produce department— just be sure to wash all samples, whack on a condom, and don't push anything too far up the butt, as we have yet to meet a cucumber with a flared base. **Acrylic** dildos like the **Lumina Wand** or blinged-out **glass** dildos are completely hard and therefore best used for very controlled play only—i.e., handheld. See **glass** for more on glass dildos; see also **VixSkin** in **dildos, realistic** on page 64.

dildos, nonrealistic

Nonrealistic dildos are usually made of **silicone**, they might be purple or green, they might curve significantly for **G-spot** or **prostate** action, and they usually taper to a point for easy entry. Some might even feature very unnatural ripples or bumps for added stimulation during thrusting. A classic in this genre is VC's Willow dildo ($$), which curves rather significantly for **G-** and **P-spot** stimulation. Its modest proportions (4^{13}⁄$_{16}$ inches by 1^{13}⁄$_{16}$ inches) and tapered end make it a great choice for beginners. Another VC option is the shortish and fattish (4^{13}⁄$_{16}$ inches by 1^{3}⁄$_{8}$ inches) Stimulator ($$), which curves slightly and features a rounded, rather than pointy, tip. Two of VC's top sellers are best described as semi-realistic: The Leo (7 inches by 1^{1}⁄$_{2}$ inches) and the Mistress (6 inches by 1^{3}⁄$_{16}$ inches). Both feature smooth shafts, gentle curves, and "proper" heads, yet they can be ordered in "glitter"

D

or "two-color swirl," too. And look, ma—no veins! Available almost everywhere ($$).

dildos, realistic

How much would you like your dildo to resemble a penis? VC's Tex dildo ($$$; BF calls it Boitoy and sells it for a little less; illustrated) is about as realistic as dildos come. It's made of their very own **VixSkin**—it's got the fleshy feel of **Cyberskin** but is actually 100 percent **silicone**, with all of silicone's benefits (ingenious!). Tex is pale peach and a pleasantly average 5 inches by 1 13/16 inches. It has a gentle curve and a very penis-esque head (i.e., it's not pointy, and it's got a frenulum instead of a face). Some backdoor beginners might find this kind of dildo a little tricky to take in because the head doesn't taper, but vaginas and seasoned butt pirates will enjoy the grand entrance made by this realistically bulbous head. It's sturdy enough to work in a **harness**, but it's soft and lifelike enough

to double as a **softpack** (with semi-chub)! Or check out BL's Ultraskin dildo ($$$): This one comes with blue veins and spongy balls, and is made of a hybrid of silicone and PVC, which is hardier than Cyberskin (but still **porous** and **phthalate**-y). GV's El Rey ($$, peach or black) is not quite as lifelike, but it *is* 100 percent silicone. Yay! Slightly *un*realistically, the Ultraskin and El Rey both feature a suction-cup base—but, hey, who's counting?

dildos, sizes of

Okay, so, ahem, size *does* matter. A little bit. But just because you *can* go large doesn't mean →

you should. We're going to go out on a limb here and say that VC's veiny, wrinkled 7½-inch (plus balls) Johnny dildo (BL, BF, GV, VC, WT; $$$) is something you should work up to. Be careful of buying long if your dildo is mostly meant for the vagina, especially if it's a dildo with a pointy end that might poke at her cervix (yowza!). Vaginas like girth. Bums, on the other hand, can handle plenty of *length*; it's the girth they need to work up to. Plus, don't forget that dildos have to travel past a few inches of ass cheek before getting in, so a too-short dildo can easily pop out of a bum (and, if you're not careful, you'll shoot your eye out). Once your dildo is strapped into a **harness**, you'll lose about half an inch, so bear that in mind as you're holding up your test-run cucumber to various silicone schlongs. If you're starting really small (like Vixen's winsomely named Willie, a mere 4¹³⁄₁₆ inches by 1 inch, available everywhere; $) be sure to go with the Terra Firma harness, as it's the most adjustable. Though, at that size, you may

find that a harness doesn't give you enough control, in which case you'll have to use your hand in conjunction or instead.

dildos, vibrating

Vibrating **dildos**, like the **silicone** Echo by **Tantus** (BL, BF, GV; about $$), have a hole in the base for inserting a **miniature vibrator**. If one is worn as a **strap-on**, the vibrations can be felt by the penetrator as well as the receiver—*such* a giver! You could also make your vibrating dildo do double duty as an external vibrator (see **vibrators, external**), if you're a one-size-fits-all kind of shopper. Dildos made of 100 percent silicone with stowaway vibrators are easier to clean than most vibes (just pop out the miniature vibrator and boil the silicone part). When the vibe motor eventually kicks the bucket (as all battery-operated toys do, sooner rather than later) you can just replace that little **bullet**,

D

which costs less than ten bucks, instead of having to replace the whole toy. For info on whether you should go with a cordless bullet or one with a separate battery pack, see **miniature vibrators**. See also the vibrating **Feeldoe double dildos**.

availability, or because your local sex-toy store is attended by sleazy men in raincoats and the only toys they sell are the **California Exotics Novelties** brand. See **blindfolds**, **chopsticks**, **ice**, **lube**, **paddles**, and **rope** for some ideas. ❷ Slang term for masturbation.

D

dirty talk

It's the cheapest **DIY** sex accessory out there. Don't believe us? Next time you're in the mood for some light **BDSM** and you can't find your rope, just tell your partner exactly what you *won't* do to them if they move so much as an inch. Be sure to go into sordid detail, using lots of four-letter words. We guarantee it'll hold better than Alabama police-issue **cuffs**.

DIY (do-it-yourself)

❶ When you make your own sex toys, whether out of desperation, thrift, creativity, need, lack of

Divine-Interventions .com

The most offensive, blasphemous, and ingenious online retailer of handcrafted and hand-colored silicone **dildos**: "Home of the Baby Jesus Butt Plug!" We shit you not. Nothing we write could be funnier than their own product descriptions, so, without further ado—Jackhammer Jesus (illustrated): "Jesus was a carpenter; now he's a powertool." The Virgin Mary dildo: "Like most smart women, Mary knows there's a Second Coming . . . and a third . . . and a fourth. And, with the Holy Lube, you betcha

→

these ain't gonna be immaculate." The Judas dildo: "Our boy sold Jesus for thirty silver pieces, and we're selling him for *even less*! If he could fuck the Son of God, imagine what he could do to you! Judas, the only non-believer of the bunch, will make a believer out of you." Yes, we know: We're going to hell.

Doc Johnson manufacturers

The biggest manufacturer of adult **novelties** in the world. They've been around for more than thirty years, making tons o' money with the quantity-over-quality model. Still, they've got some popular products that work well, like the **Pocket Rocket vibrator** and the similar iVibes series (BF, MP). And they're the exclusive makers of Vivid-**porn-star**-branded items.

double dildos

See **dildos, double**; **Feeldoe**; and **Nexus**.

douche, anal

Some serious butt pirates refuse to use the servant's entrance until they've douched back there. *We* say, what's wrong with a daily dose of fiber and a good shower beforehand? An anal douche, sometimes called an enema, is meant to ease constipation or just get you squeaky-clean back there: You inject a solution into the anus, hold it for a few minutes, then open the floodgates. That doesn't sound much like foreplay to us, but if *you* think it does, check out a book called *Intimate Invasion: The Erotic*

Ins & Outs of Enema Play, by M. R. Strict, for advice we're too squeamish to give.

FYI, the chemicals in enema solutions can irritate the anal lining, so, if you *must* do it, at least dump the solution and use warm water instead. However, some studies have shown that any kind of enema, even just a plain water douche, can increase the likelihood of HIV transmission once you get to the sex. Plus, as with laxatives, your bowels can get hooked on enemas. So why not just stick a soapy finger where the sun don't shine and repeat as necessary (be sure to rinse thoroughly afterward, because soap residue can be irritating back there). If you're really set on that final rinse cycle, the only product we can *kind* of get behind, as it were, is the cheery-looking small plastic anal douche sold for about ten bucks (BL, LB). It basically works like a big syringe—use it to gently squirt a little warm water up there after a BM. And eat your Bran Flakes, already. See also **anal play**.

douche, vaginal

Don't go there. The vagina is not supposed to smell like a "summer's eve." It's supposed to smell like a vagina, people! And, believe it or not, someone who is attracted to a vagina owner tends to *like* the smell of that woman's healthy vagina. We actually find it hard to believe these products are still on the market, considering that they've been linked to pelvic inflammatory disease, infertility, and ectopic pregnancy. Plus, douches can upset the balance of your natural, good bacteria down there, actually *creating* a bad smell once all that fake

→

D

eau-de-meadow bouquet wears off. And, while we're on the subject, the perfume and detergents in those "vagina sprays" can be extremely irritating, too. Stop the madness! If you're self-conscious, by all means shower before sex—we all feel more comfortable having our various nooks and crannies explored after a good, soapy rubdown. If you still smell kind of funky down there, it could indicate some kind of vaginal infection, in which case you should see your doc. Or it could just mean that you should wear looser pants and cotton undies, drink more water and less coffee, eat better, and stop smoking. Do you *really* need that much Lycra in your wardrobe? See also **vaginal canal**.

Drugstore.com (DS)

Hello? They sell like a hundred vibrators! Who says sex toys haven't gone mainstream? Of course, you won't find **butt plugs** or **spreader bars** here. The great thing about Drugstore.com is that they organize their items by manufacturer and actually use the manufacturer-given toy name. Plus, all the accompanying images of **dildos** and the like feature a 2-inch daisy beside them, not only to provide you with a size comparison, but also to give your sex-toy shopping experience a kinder, gentler feel.

D

dual-action

Dual-action **vibrators** are designed to simultaneously stimulate a woman's **clitoris** *and* the **vaginal canal** (usually the **G-spot**). Double whammy! Dual-action vibes reviewed in this book include the **Rabbit Habit & the Rabbit Pearl** (the entry includes reviews of multiple dual-action vibes), the **Rock Chick**, the Ultime (see **Natural Contours toys**), and the absolutely massive **Thunder Cloud**. A.k.a. twice-as-nice vibes. See also **triple-action**.

Duckie water-proof vibrator

A cute little yellow "rubber" duckie that doubles as a water-proof vibe. No wonder *Sesame Street*'s Ernie was obsessed with his! This battery-operated, super-quiet toy goes by different nicknames, depending on which store you visit—I Rub My Duckie on BF and GV, the Ducky Vibe on BL, the Lucky Duck on MP, etc. ($). Comes in lavender, black, travel size, a devil costume, or a **BDSM** version complete with duckie **gimp suit**! GV and BF sell all these variations, plus Duckie's friends I Rub My Wormie and I Rub My Fishie. If you like your orgasms on the philanthropic side, get your Duckie at **Blowfish**—they donate 5 percent of every sale to the International Bird Rescue Research Center, in Fairfield, California. Made of **phthalate**-free **PVC**, Duckie is **porous**, so don't share Duckie with more than one friend, no matter how many times he or she shares a bubble bath with you! See also **bath accessories** and **water-proof toys**.

duotone (and tritone) balls

Like **Ben Wa balls**, only meatier. Usually slightly bigger than the Ben Wa kind, duotone and tritone balls are connected by a cord and have a loose weight inside each of the two (duotone) or three (tritone) hollow spheres, causing subtle vibrations against the vaginal walls when you move (some free-floating Ben Was are similarly weighted, instead of solid). Depending on the make, the weights inside each ball may knock or jingle audibly (though, admittedly, the sound is muf-fled). It's a little like carrying →

a bag of marbles in your body cavity. To help turn it up a notch, you can play around with insertion and removal, keep one ball on the outside for external stim, or use a strong external vibrator like the **Hitachi** to get things shaking. Unfortunately, many of these products are cheaply produced, with plastic seams and absorbent strings, both of which can foster bad bacterial growth. Better to go with balls and cords that are coated in **silicone**, hard **elastomer** (like **Smartballs**), or at least **latex**. And unless it's made specifically for the caboose, we'd keep it away from your tush. Available as the Private Reserve on MP ($).

E

edible accessories

Haven't you ever had the urge to take a vat of room-temperature Smart Balance Buttery Spread, get naked with your partner, and wrestle? Well, make your dreams come true with a vinyl **sheet**. Or simply jump in the shower. Just be sure to keep any foodstuffs away from sensitive **vaginas**, which are prone to infections and allergic reactions. There are plenty of digestible products to choose from, like edible **massage oil**, warming fluid, **lube**, and **body paint**, most of which taste like shit. But going **DIY** isn't always the best-laid plan to get laid, either. For instance, smearing your honey in honey or chocolate syrup may sound sinful and sumptuous in theory, but in practice it's a terribly uncomfortable, sticky situation.

Instead, try anything from one of the best, most sophisticated names in edible products, **Kama Sutra**: They've got **Honey Dust** (see **massage oil, body**); a Lover's Paintbox, with dark, milk, and white chocolate "paints"; massage creams in flavors like honey almond and raspberry crème; latex-compatible Oils of Love; and erogenous-zone-safe Pleasure Balm, which is reminiscent of mint spice drops—none of which will trigger your gag reflex. They're all available from BF at tastefully affordable prices. Or try GV's oil-based, petroleum-free, and **vegan** Body Butter massage balm, in mint julep or raspberry-chocolate truffle, or their Body Candy, in strawberry champagne, thin mint, and toasted coconut. And you can get a Chocoholics Chocolate Shower Bar at most online wedding-favor shops for about five bucks. Then, of course, there are the really mature **novelties** that you aren't actually supposed to play with, like Macweenie & Cheese, Boob Pasta, Hard Pecker Candy, etc. (GV). Our faves are the penis- and boobie-shaped cupcake pans (GV), which give us a cozy Betty Crackwhore feeling.

edible underwear

You probably received this Fruit Roll-up wannabe as a **gag gift** at a **bachelorette party** a few years back. The thought of putting something sticky and cherry flavored against your cooch was so unpleasant that you shoved it all the way to the back of your undies drawer, where it passed its sell-by date and congealed itself onto your favorite black lace bra.

elastomer

Elastomer is an umbrella term for various polymers with the elastic properties of natural rubber. So this *could* include **Cyberskin**, **jelly**, **latex**, **silicone**, and **vinyl** (including PVC). *However,* in the sex-toy industry, the word is usually used to refer to thermoplastic elastomer (TPE) →

E

or thermoplastic rubber (TPR). The chemical process involved in making TPE is different from that of **vinyl** and **jelly**, so the resulting product is **phthalate** free and latex free (woo-hoo!). Even Greenpeace recommends it as a better alternative to PVC.

It can be manipulated into a wide variety of textures much more easily than silicone, and with varying porosity. For example, **Vibratex** has a new generation of phthalate- and latex-free soft toys (see **Rabbit Habit & Rabbit Pearl vibrators** for examples) made from this material, which they're simply calling elastomer. This soft elastomer (like Vibratex's **Pixie vibrator**) is super squishy and **porous** (unlike silicone), which means you should use a condom to keep it bacteria free and wash it with mild soap and water.

But elastomers can also be hard and **nonporous** (like **Fun Factory**'s **Smartballs**), which means you can forgo the condom and wash it in the top rack of your dishwasher. Fun Factory has trademarked their hard, nontoxic, hypoallergenic ver-

sion of TPE as Elastomed, but because there are no industry standards for the materials of sex toys or the terms used to describe them, any manufacturer can use the word *elastomer* to describe a toy that might have phthalates or latex in it. Similarly, because elastomers can be silicone based, manufacturers can promote a product as silicone, even though it's got other stuff in it that makes it porous. Buyer beware.

E

Elemental Pleasures.com (manufacturers)

Makers of the relatively new, **high-end**, handcrafted, American-made **vibrator** series: Léopard (made from posh stainless steel), Le Tigre (light-blue, anodized, aircraft-grade aluminum), Le Lynx (medical-grade titanium), and Panthere (pink, anodized, aircraft-grade aluminum). They each come with three swappable tips, multiple speed settings, and a silver

→

attaché case with velvet lining and lock and key. They're all "hot tub safe" (i.e., **waterproof**), boilable for sanitation, and pretty darn quiet for the crazy-intense vibrations they give off. Use them externally or internally: EP says you can use them either vaginally or anally; *we* say, these vibes don't have a flared base, so keep 'em out of your butt. Founders and "Supreme Commanders" Peg and Dennis are both degreed mechanical engineers who spent fifteen years designing and manufacturing components for commercial aircraft(!). And, with a starting price of $250, they're coming close to airplane sticker prices. Too bad their choice of an animal-print design theme on the packaging cheapens them a tad.

Emotional Bliss toys

This line of U.K. **contour toys** is distributed exclusively in the United States by GV. Like **Natural Contours toys**, they're sleek, discreet (they look like cosmetic products!), and ergonomically designed (all can be controlled by the light touch of a finger). They're also, like, three times as expensive as Natural Contours products. For that you get medical-grade materials and a *forty-five-speed* control, and they're all rechargeable! (Most of the toys last sixty to ninety minutes after a twelve-hour charge; the finger toys last three hours when fully charged.)

The Femblossom ($$$$) covers most of the vulva—imagine a hand cupped to hold water—for gentle, generalized vibes. It's great for sensitive-ponytail clits and women who like a little attention paid to the labes. Jasmine ($$$$) looks like a woman's electric shaver and is meant for more direct clitoral stimulation. Womolia ($$$$) vibrates either externally

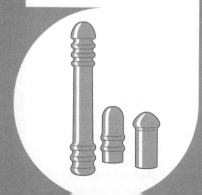

→

or just in the first few inches of the vagina—i.e., the most sensitive part. Finally, Isis ($$$) and the slightly larger and more vigorous Chandra ($$$) are Emotional Bliss's answer to **finger toys**. Each one comes with three finger bands so you can find the perfect fit (or share the toy with your big-handed rugby-player boyfriend). Emotional Bliss toys are made of medical-grade, **nonporous** thermoplastic **elastomer**, and you can clean them by wiping with a damp, soapy cloth. There's more info at EmotionalBliss.com, though you can buy them only via **Good Vibrations**. See also **rechargeable toys**.

ErosBoutique .com (EB)

A good place to get all your **BDSM** gear, when the **blindfold** you got free on your transatlantic flight just won't cut it. You want hog-tie **cuffs**, **collars** with attached **nipple clamps**, impression **paddles** that leave the word *slut* imprinted on your tush, a catsuit, or a **gimp suit**? They've got it. A better selection than EX, but quite a bit pricier. Plus, some of their descriptions aren't exactly delicate ("great for pounding your cock into your partner" or "tonsil diving"). Their retail shop is located in Boston's South End, for all your south end's needs.

Eroscillator 2 Plus vibrator

This old-school, ugly-ass **vibrator** is the only sex toy ever endorsed by Dr. Ruth. It looks like a cross between an electric toothbrush and something a Victorian doctor might have

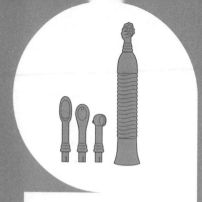

used to treat **hysteria**. And the packaging would be more fitting for a *Star Wars* figurine. But who says all sex toys have to be pretty in pink? The nifty thing about this copper-colored plastic toy is that it *oscillates* instead of vibrating—i.e., it moves kind of like your electric toothbrush. (And don't tell us you've never made bedroom eyes at your Sonicare on a quiet night in.) This means it's less vigorous than something like the **Hitachi**, so it's less likely to cause a numb **clitoris**.

This toy comes with three power settings and three interchangeable heads the manufacturer describes with the trademarked term *flabbergasmic*. (Hey, you'd trademark that, too,

if you came up with it.) These heads are all designed for labia or clit stimulation and include a Golden Spoon attachment that is scooped out like the **Clitoral Hummer waterproof vibrator** and serves a similar purpose. If you spring for the more expensive version of the toy, the Eroscillator Top Deluxe, you'll also get an insertion attachment called the Seven Pearls of the Orient and something dubbed the French Legionnaire's Moustache, which basically turns your toy into a vibrating false moustache. (The perfect accessory for watching some vintage seventies porn!)

The Eroscillator is one of the few plug-in vibes that's made specifically for naughty doings (unlike all those **"back" massagers**, whose manufacturers tend to be more coy about things). Lightweight, quiet, and easy to hold, this toy doesn't get too warm, its 12-foot cord is handy if your bedroom is outlet challenged, and the toy is svelte enough to fit between two partners during intercourse. We've come a long way, baby, but don't

E

→

knock old-school until you've tried it. Clean your Eroscillator with a damp washcloth (the toy is **waterproof**, but the plug and converter aren't, obviously). Available at most places, including Eroscillator.com ($$$$; the more powerful Deluxe model is about $30 more).

erotic furniture

Remember that scene in *Harold & Maude* when she tells him to "stroke, palm, caress, *explore*" her 5-foot wooden sculpture and he puts his head in its hole like he's performing arboreal cunnilingus? That piece would pass as erotic furniture. It's pretty much anything that's bigger than a bread box and is designed specifically for sexual purposes, like water-resistant foam Liberator wedges and ramps (that lift one's pelvis or butt for easier penetration or oral sex; available everywhere), **swings** and **slings**, fucking machines, the **Bodybouncer**, **queening stools**, **BDSM** bondage beds, stocks and pillories, racks, "surgical" tables, and maybe that futon you had in college that you could convert into a bed with one foot while you were lying down and making out on it with someone.

etiquette, gift-giving

We happen to think that sex toys make great gifts (*way* better than lingerie), but there's a world of difference between an unassuming soft **jelly** vibrating cock **ring** and a 7½-inch veiny **dildo** called Johnny, even if you do tie a pink ribbon around it. **Kits** tend to make great gifts, because they're nicely packaged and they're typically **beginner** friendly. If the gift is for your partner, toys you can share— like a **bath accessory**—are a pretty safe bet, too. And little toys, like **miniature-vibrator** accessories or **finger toys**, are less scary to newbies. If it's a toy for a friend, try an **undercover toy** like a vibrating lipstick— that way, they can always choose to accept it in jest, if they're embarrassed. But there's no guarantee your partner won't freak out and say, "You think I *need* this?" or "What kind of perv do you take me for?" (If your friend reacts that way, just give them this book and tell them what nice girls we are, and that they should just get over themselves and enjoy the gift.)

Don't give a "gift" that's obviously a present to yourself, like polyester butt-floss lingerie that may look good to you but feels terribly uncomfortable to the person you're supposed to be pampering. (Make requests for that kind of thing on your *own* birthday.) And make sure the present you're giving is appropriate to the person: A **leather** harness for the **vegan** in your life or a PVC dildo for a beloved environmentalist probably won't be well received (you may as well get them fruitcake while you're at it). Shopping *together* might be a better idea— it means they get to pick out something they truly want. Take them to a clean, well-lit sex-toy shop with helpful staff, like **Babeland** or **Good Vibrations**,

or a **high-end sex toy** boutique, like Kiki de Montparnasse (Kikidm.com), or log on to one of their Web sites together. See also **communication**; **etiquette, recycling**.

etiquette, recycling

We're often asked if it's okay to "reuse" a sex toy that outlasts the relationship it was originally purchased for. This rarely happens with battery-operated vibrators, as their shelf life is so limited, but it's often an issue with something more hardy, like a **silicone** dildo. If you're only going to reuse it on yourself, fine: Go nuts. But if you're thinking of reusing it with a *new* partner? Our answer is always no. We don't care how "hygienic" silicone is or how it's "totally safe if you boil it for a few minutes on the stove top": That's just plain disrespectful, in our book (the one you're holding *and* our metaphorical book). It's kind of like recycling the sex-mix tape that your first true love made

→

for you (please don't tell us you've ever done that). We know sex toys are expensive—but, hey, hearts are precious, too, and we break those all the time.

If you're *convinced* your partner is cool enough to be down with sloppy seconds and you're totally broke and you think our rule is stupid, go ahead and ask nicely. (But just in case you're wrong, here's one for the road: *We told you so*.)

Regifting is cool only if the toy has never been used—and we're talking not even out of its packaging. Who wants a toy that's been manhandled, possibly dropped on the floor, or even licked by your dog?

The only exception to these etiquette guidelines is this: You have a toy you've only ever used on yourself before that you'd like to introduce to your partner. Hey, some people need a helping hand to get off, even if they've got a partner with two willing, working hands. And your toy might very well be one of those **high-end sex toys** that's worth at least half a pair of Manolos. You might be quite

nervous about admitting your electronic needs to your partner, since doing so can feel like the equivalent of sharing a family secret or confessing to a love of reality TV. If this is the case, only an asshole would demand that you throw the toy out the window. But if the partner in question would simply prefer you not use your old standby in their presence and then offers to replace your toy with a brand-new equivalent model— at least for your couple time— well, that's just dandy.

EvesGarden .com

Founded in 1974 by women's rights activist Dell Williams, Eve's Garden is the world's first mail-order catalogue and sexuality boutique designed specifically for women. You won't find any **gag gifts** in their midtown Manhattan store, which feels quiet and clinical, kind of like a doctor's office (especially because it's discreetly located on the upper levels of an office building). Eve's Garden takes sexual fun very seriously. After all, the eighty-three-year-old founder still believes that a woman who is unfettered sexually is unfettered politically, socially, and economically. Amen, sister!

extenders, penis

Sheaths worn by the male member to add girth, length, and texture (because you wouldn't want a *real* penis to come with raised bumps along the shaft that look contagious). Great for the receiver looking for a change of pace; bad for the wearer who hopes to feel anything during penetration. Of course, that might be just what the sex doctor ordered for chronic premature ejaculators. **Vibratex** makes variously shaped Crystal Sleeves (sold as the Chief on LB; $$). *Not* to be used as contraception or STD protection. A.k.a. penis **sleeves**, **French ticklers**.

Extreme Restraints.com (EX)

Looking for the best deal on a **leather** horse muzzle for your loved one? You've come to the right place. EX has got better selections and prices than your general sex-toy shops for **BDSM** paraphernalia, though their safety and material info on each accessory often leaves something to be desired. And though their site looks slightly more hardcore than the fetish emporium **ErosBoutique.com** (maybe it's the large shackled man screaming on their home page), ExtremeRestraints.com's prices are much, much softer.

F

Feeldoe double dildos

Tantus's number-one best seller, the Feeldoe is your sure thing if you want to go hands and **harness** free while fucking your boyfriend or girlfriend with a **silicone** dong. It'll still take a bit of practice—and regular **kegel** exercises—to get it right. In fact, some people prefer to steady their Feeldoe with a harness, tighty-whities, or a helping hand. But the Feeldoe has been specially designed to stay put. The driver's end of the Feeldoe is bulbous and weighted, to help with stability and **G-spot** stimulation. Plus, three small ridges, located where the two halves meet in the middle, provide clitoral stimulation.

The other end of the Feeldoe, a.k.a. the poking end, curves up slightly (like an erect penis might) and can be inserted into either another vagina or an asshole (the body part, we mean). Feeldoe drivers *can* use it in *their* butts, too, but it was designed by a woman *for* women and their partners. The steep angle (45 degrees) of this dildo makes it perfect for face-to-face, harness-free sex.

This double-happiness dildo comes in three models: the Feeldoe, the Feeldoe Slim, and the Feeldoe Stout. The original Feeldoe can be bought with or without a **miniature vibrator** in the elbow joint; the Feeldoe Slim automatically comes with a miniature vibe. The driver's end of any kind of Feeldoe is 2½ inches long and 1½ inches wide. The poking end of the original model is 6 inches long and 1½ inches wide. The Feeldoe Slim is ideal for butt beginners: The poking end is 5½ inches long and just over 1¼ inches wide. The Feeldoe Stout's poker is 5¾ inches by 1¾ inches.

For more info and inspirational Maya Angelou quotes (no, seriously), check out Feeldoe.com, where you'll also learn that the plural of Feeldoe is Feeldoe. You know, like the deer.

→

The Feeldoe is made of pure **silicone**, so it can be washed or boiled—be sure to remove the vibe first! And don't forget to buy some water-based **lube**. Available all over (BL calls it the Divining Rod, and WT calls the original the Cagney & Lacey and the slim one the Kate & Allie; $$$). See also **dildos**; **dildos, double**; **harnesses**; and **strap-ons**.

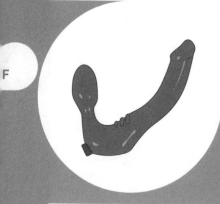

fetish play & gear

See **BDSM**.

finger cots/ finger condoms

Latex sheaths for individual fingers that are smaller and thicker than regular condoms. Handy if you have fingers with cuts, if you're grossed out by anything you might run into in an orifice, if you want a smoother entry (especially anally), if you have long or jagged fingernails, or if you like to wear Lee Press-Ons.

finger toys

One of the only complaints we ever hear about vibrators is that they can make you feel a bit distant from the whole orgasm process. Like you may as well get maintenanced by a cold, impersonal fucking machine while you read the paper or do the dishes. And how many guys, on first being introduced to their girlfriend's **Rabbit Habit**, have pouted and

→

said, "Well, I don't see why you need *me* around"? Sure, you could hand over the control panel or buy a **remote control toy**, but that doesn't change the fact that when you're using a vibrator, your own hand can't really *feel* what you're doing.

But what if you could let your fingers do the walking, like the good folks at the Yellow Pages always say? What if your fingers could vibrate at approximately the same frequency as a **Hitachi Magic Wand**? Enter—cue the singing angels—finger toys!

A finger toy, sometimes called a finger extension, is basically a finger-size vibrator covered in a soft sheath that straps onto your own finger. **Lube** it up, turn it on, and carry on doing whatever you would usually do with your hands during sex—handwork for her, hand job for him, **perineum** massage for either, etc. (Note: Finger toys are for *external* use only.) You can strap the toy onto the fingertip side for direct application, or you can swing it around to the knuckle side so it's your own vibrating finger that's touching down on yours or your partner's genitals. Either way, you'll get much more subtlety and range of motion than you do with a regular ol' **vibrator**—it's like someone replaced one of your fingers with a vibrating prosthetic. And who could possibly feel trumped by their own prosthetic digit?

Finger toys are quiet and inconspicuous, which makes them great for couples play. The mack daddy of finger toys is undoubtedly the **Fukuoku 9000**, though a few other manufacturers are starting to get in on the game. Finger Fun (BL; $) is bulkier than the Fukuoku, so it's better suited for foreplay or solo play rather than during intercourse, but it does have the benefit of being **waterproof**. Or, if you want to get fancy, the **high-end sex toy** company **Emotional Bliss** makes two ergonomically designed, *rechargeable* finger toys: Isis (GV; $$$) and the slightly larger, slightly pricier Chandra (GV).

F

Fireman's Pump

It's a penis pump designed to look like—you got it!—a fireman's pump. "For the man who wants a real fire hose!" the packaging promises. Well, you know our position on **pumps, penis**. But if you really *must* indulge, what better excuse than to "put out a really big fire"? Where's your truck, big boy? A **California Exotics Novelties** product, natch, cheapest at DS ($).

Fleshlight

The king of **masturbation sleeves**, if only for its great gimmick factor: It's shaped like a gigantic flashlight, but there's **Cyberskin**-esque material sculpted into a mouth, vagina, anus, or coin slot on the business end (i.e., where the bulb would be). You get to choose whether the 10-inch canal is ribbed, bumpy, tight, ultratight, or wavy. And it's available in pink, mocha, ice, and gold. Though the Fleshlight is one of the most—if not *the* most—popular men's toys, you might find the flashlight casing heavy, unwieldy, and too wide. Plus, you can't squeeze the casing to increase the pressure around your dick. If that's the case, you can remove the sleeve in order to better manipulate the fleshy canal with your hands. Just make sure you remove the hard stabilizing tube from the inside before you go poking away! It's available everywhere, though you can get the most customization for the least amount of money ($$) on Fleshlight.com.

→

But, frankly, the less gimmicky Dream Sleeve (MP) and GV's exclusive Ecsta-Sleeve (with miniature vibe!) will both cost you less and give you more.

Flexi Felix anal beads (on a stalk)

Did you ever meet a sex toy so damn cute you wanted to cuddle with it more than you wanted to fuck it? That's the Flexi Felix, a caterpillar whose funny little head features a shy smile, dinky feelers, and two holes for your fingers—all the better to pull Felix out of your lover's asshole with. The FF is a modern take on **anal beads** by **Fun Factory**. It's 12 inches long and consists of five 100 percent **silicone** beads (ranging in width from ¾ inch to 1 inch) attached to a bendy stalk. As the Flexi Felix is inserted into the anus, the beads will nestle together in a cozy bundle, creating a comfortably full feeling (as opposed to the uncomfortably invasive feeling 12 inches would give you in a straight line). Felix comes in black, blue, or pink (because even girly-girls like to entertain backdoor friends). Wash by hand, throw it in the dishwasher, or boil. Available almost everywhere ($$).

F

floggers

Paddles, slappers, **riding crops**, **canes**, **whips**, belts, or anything else used to spank a partner in a sexual scenario. As with any toy intended to inflict a sort of pleasurable pain, do your homework on safety measures and proper technique to avoid serious or permanent injury. FYI, some people also use *flogger* to mean a certain kind of whip—see **whips** for details. See also **BDSM** and **safe, sane & consensual**.

food play

See **edible accessories**.

French ticklers

Cheaply made **extenders**. See also **sleeves**.

Fukuoku 9000 finger toy

Don't be fooled by the packaging: Though the Fukuoku 9000 claims to ease "muscle tension, headaches, eye fatigue, and sinus pain," it's actually *the* **finger toy** for sex on the market. And, in fact, if you read the Fukuoku instruction book closely enough, you'll notice the coy "for enjoyment with your friends and companions" suggestion. (Heh-heh, they said "companions.")

The Fukuoku 9000 is, hands down (sorry), the best finger toy to use during sex. The ol' reach-around? How about the brand-new, *vibrating* reach-around? You decide. The F-9000 consists of one vibrating plastic →

finger strap and four variously textured jelly sleeves to slide over it (though they all feel pretty much the same, if you ask us). Your Fukuoku should be **monogamous**. Plus, don't use it internally, and wipe it clean with a little alcohol on a cloth between uses. Available everywhere! BF is cheapest, at under twenty bucks.

And, while we're at it, we should introduce you to the extended Fukuoku family. The Fukuoku Power Pack ($$) is basically three Fukuoku 9000s connected to a battery pack that straps to your wrist. And then there's the Fukuoku Massage Glove ($$), a soft, washable glove, available in either lefty or righty, with a teeny **vibrator** embedded in each fingertip. Hello, hand job!

Fun Factory

The Germans make great cars, so it follows that they'd make great sex toys. Located at FunFactory.de, they're kicking serious butt in the biz these days, manufacturing nontoxic, odorless, 100 percent hypoallergenic, easy-to-clean, whisper-quiet, ergonomic toys like the **Laya Spot vibrator** and **Flexi Felix anal beads**, made from either medical-grade **silicone** or **nonporous**, **phthalate**-free, hard **elastomer**, which they have trademarked as Elastomed. Plus, their products work wonderfully and feel fantastic—you can't really get any better than that these days. Their tagline is "Love Yourself," and they believe that doing so should be as normal as going to the grocery store. Their toys actually come with helpful instruction manuals—unheard of with **novelties**. Yes, their brightly colored designs, cutesy inchworm faces, and smiling dolphins will remind you of *Sesame Street* and kids' beach paraphernalia

F

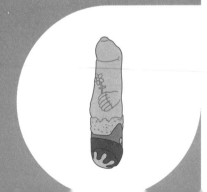

(Exhibit A: Their squinty-eyed, flower-holding Dinky Digger illustrated on previous page), but maybe that's what makes these vibes so approachable: They're cheery!

Mainstream department stores all over Europe such as Galleries Lafayette, Printemps, and Otto carry FF items, and even **high-end** Henri Bendel, on 5th Avenue in New York, have sold their **Smartballs**. Check out their rechargeable vibes with docking stations and their line of Astro Toys, one vibe for each sign of the Zodiac (great b-day gifts). Available most everywhere, though many places rename them ($$-$$$). See also **G-Swirl & G-Twist vibrators**.

G

G-spot, hers

The spongy tissue surrounding her urethra that can be felt through the top wall of the vagina, about 2 inches inside. Some doctors consider this area the female **prostate**. For some women, it's the key to orgasm (or another key besides the **clitoris**) and even female ejaculation. Since those things often require firm, steady, extended pressure that a penis or even a hand can't manage for too long, many sex toys have been made specifically to target the G-spot (see **G-spot stimulators**). However, it's worth noting—before you start demanding your money back on your **G-spotter**—that some women feel nothing at all when this area is poked, while others find it annoying (as in, it makes them want to pee), or even painful.

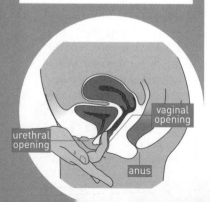

F

G-spot, his

The prostate gland. For more details, see **P-spot**.

G-spot stimulators (his & hers)

If a toy is meant to be inserted and it's got a curve to it, chances are it has G-spot stimulation (either his or hers) on the brain. However, toys that are curved but don't have a flared base should *not* be used up the bum, as they might get lost. This includes boomerangs. Male-specific G-toys targeting the **prostate** (or **P-spot**) can usually be used by women, either in the tush (where they won't find a prostate) or in the vagina (where they may find their G-spot). Just don't swap between orifices without a thorough cleaning first.

G-Spotter (brand name)

See **Hitachi Magic Wand attachments**.

G-spotters (variety of toy)

Toys intended to target a woman's G-spot.

G-Swirl & G-Twist Vibrators

Designed and sold by **Good Vibrations** and produced by

→

Fun Factory, these vibrating **G-spotters** are big sellers. Here's why: sleek design, quiet, **waterproof**, hypoallergenic, **nonporous**, **latex** free, **phthalate** free, and **silicone**. Just *reading* an impressive list like that gives us a mini orgasm. They each take two AA batteries (included by GV); $$.

gag gifts

Any sex accessory primarily intended to elicit laughter rather than genuine desire, such as **edible underwear**, gold-lamé thongs for dudes, mac & cheese with penis-shaped pasta, and anything listed under **bachelorette-party paraphernalia**. If it's cheap and you'll never use it, it's a gag gift. For one small step up the evolutionary chain, see **novelties**. See also **edible accessories**.

gags, mouth

See **ball gags**.

games

Board and card games centered on sex don't just facilitate fun, they can also impart sexual knowledge, add spice, and improve **communication** between partners, especially long-term ones. (Of course, a good ol' game of Truth or Dare might work just as well.) Store-bought fun ranges from simple trivia games to full-on orgiastic Candy Lands. One best seller is Sex Smarts, a trivia quiz using flash cards containing multiple-choice and T/F questions to test and teach people of all sexual persuasions about the history of sex, sexual slang, positions, anatomy, etc. Then there are games intended for one hetero couple, like Nookii or the elegantly packaged Eros Trix, or the position-driven Kama Sutra Game, which gives each player naughty directions (for instance, one might have to frisk the other like an inappropriate cop). Finally, for a cheap thrill that loses its novelty after about ten minutes, but is still kind of sweet in its simplicity, there's

Dirty Dice: One die names a body part and the other die tells you what to do with it (for instance: "suck/lips," or "lick/below waist"). For only a couple bucks, it makes a fun **gag gift** (available in English and Spanish; for all orientations).

Gee-Whiz

See **Hitachi Magic Wand attachments**.

gerbils

Not sex toys! We're sure you're familiar with the number-one urban legend of all time: "Richard Gere once got a gerbil stuck up his ass." Which doesn't even make sense, since the actor's a **vegetarian**. The online bullshit detector, Snopes.com, debunks this myth once and for all at Snopes.com/risque/homosex/gerbil.htm. There, you'll also find that hilarious radio clip of a DJ reading the faux news piece that detailed the same story, sans Gere. If you're

having a bad day, give it a listen: It's sure to brighten your day.

Gimp, the (as in, "Bring out the Gimp")

❶ The character clad in head-to-toe **leather** from Quentin Tarantino's 1994 movie *Pulp Fiction.* A cop named Zed and his redneck friend Maynard keep him locked in a chest in their basement. The two take Butch (Bruce Willis) and his nemesis, Marsellus (Ving Rhames), hostage and **ball-gag** them. When Butch and Marsellus awake, Zed tells Maynard, "Bring out the Gimp." It was, by far, the most quoted line from a movie that year—at least among our circle of friends.

gimp suit

❶ A full **leather** onesie complete with face mask (with two eye holes and a zipper mouth), like the one worn by the **Gimp** in *Pulp Fiction.* ❷ Any serious **BDSM** outfit.

girl's best friend

Hint: You can't buy it from DeBeers.

glass

It sounds like a really bad idea to stick something inside you that's made out of glass. But purpose-made glass **dildos** and **butt plugs** are some of the sturdiest—not to mention most beautiful—sex toys around. Put one on your mantle, and it could pass as an artsy-fartsy paper-weight. Accidentally knock it off your mantle, and it probably won't break (though if it's thrown around carelessly, it can chip and become a dagger of death, at which point it's time to say bye-bye). The firmness and weight of glass toys make them great for **kegel** exercises and **G-** or **P-spot** stimulation.

Because blown glass is seam-less and **nonporous**, a little bit of lube will make your glass toy slipperier than a seal drowning in an oil spill. It's designed to withstand heat extremes and will warm up with your body temp nicely; run it under warm water first to heat things up, or pop it in the fridge (not the freezer!) for a minute to make your own creamsicle (get it? *cream*sicle?).

Glass toys come in endless shapes and sizes. Some are perfectly clear, some have hints of color, and some even have actual artwork embedded *inside* the glass (of course, the artwork is more velvet Elvis than Picasso, but still). And if the toy is hand-blown glass (heh-heh), you know you've got a one-of-a-kind. They run the gamut from a simple $50 wand to a $700 butt plug made from obsidian (volcanic glass) by **high-end** designer Mi-Su, though with their popularity on the rise, prices are coming down. Phallix is the king of glass-dildo manufacturing and distribution. Look for the brand

→

G

name **Pyrex** (or at least a "medical-grade" description) to guarantee high-quality heat- and chemical-resistant glass. If the instructions say you can't boil it, it's not worth getting. And need we say that a glass bottle (et al.) does not a dildo make?

Good Vibrations.com (also Good Vibes.com)

The *best* sex-toy seller there is! Funky, sophisticated design; thorough product info; responsible health info; high-quality product selection; and a healthy sense of progressive inclusion. They take what they do *very* seriously but somehow manage to keep it fun and cheese free. They have a line of about eighty GV-branded products: Most are just high-quality toys you can get elsewhere, with the GV stamp of approval and funky GV packaging. But about twenty are GV originals—like the Ecsta-Sleeve **masturbation**

sleeve and the **G-Swirl & G-Twist**—designed by their trained staff (which includes their sexologist goddess, Carol Queen, PhD, the nicest woman in the sex biz) in conjunction with accomplished manufacturers like **Fun Factory**. They've even got an online magazine, an in-store Antique Vibrator Museum, and an online video rental service that's as easy as Netflix (do you really need to <u>own</u> *The Devil in Mrs. Jones*?).

Sex therapist and educator Joani Blank says she founded Good Vibrations in San Francisco almost thirty years ago because women didn't have a comfortable place to shop for sex-related products (except for New York's **Eve's Garden**). But, almost immediately, men started showing up to ask, "Can I shop here, too? I don't like those other places, either." So GV stocked men's products over time and eventually began hiring men. Just recently they've been noted as the largest employer of transgendered people in San Francisco (their other retail stores are located in Berkeley,

➔

CA and Brookline, MA). And they've got a legacy, too: Former GV interns and employees went on to open women-oriented **Babeland**, **Grand Opening**, and **Vixen Creations**. And, finally, they're one of only two shops that sent us two—count 'em, *two*—sets of toys (one for Em and one for Lo) when we requested free product samples for "research purposes" (VC was the other). See also *Bend Over Boyfriend*.

Goody Bag

Want to keep your toy snug as a bug in a rug? The Goody Bag (BF, MP, WT; $) hides your toy from prying eyes or from wandering pets who might mistake it for a chew toy. The drawstring bag is velvety on the outside and lined with waterproof nylon, to help keep the toy **clean** (or in case your toy travels with **lube** or is the "leaky" **Cyberskin** kind). The Goody Bag is machine washable and accommodates a toy up to 9 inches long. If your concern is more about protecting your **glass** dildo, check out the velvety Padded Pouch (BF; $$). If discretion is the order of the day, one of BF's travel cases ($) could pass for a shaving kit—just what you need to take your toy on the road, though of course it's no guarantee that the airport X-ray machine won't pick up on your **dildo**. For the record, we recommend checking all sex toys—especially that titanium Le Lynx, by **Elemental Pleasures**. A.k.a. toy cozies. See also **storage**.

Grand Opening.com

A cleverly named sex shop in Boston with a terribly cheesy Web site featuring lots of pictures of the owner, Kim Airs—a woman who looks more like an elementary school teacher than a "proprietrix." But once you hear her wax enthusiastic about sex, you'll be a Grand Opening believer, lame purple Web site and all.

H

hair-removal tools

Did you know that the Gillette Mach 3 Power razor *vibrates*? Don't tell us we're the only ones to think dirty thoughts when we saw that. Shaving each other down there is one of the most intimate acts a couple can share. Casual rimming is one thing, but letting someone near your private parts with a razor? Now, that takes trust. If razor blades don't sound like foreplay to you, try a buzzy electric shaver or clippers instead. And, not to get all New Age-y on you or anything, but, honestly, you'd be surprised what you can learn about your lover's genitals by getting that up close and personal. Just please approach the task with as much respect, caution, and attention to detail as a neurosurgeon would a brain op, mmkay?

handcuffs

See **cuffs**.

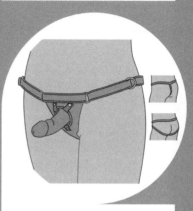

harnesses, about

If you want to go all look-ma-no-hands with your **dildo**, you're going to need a harness (unless you've got one of those newfangled strapless double dildos like the **Feeldoe** or the **Nexus**). A dildo plus a harness equals a **strap-on** (said dildo must have a flared base to hold it in place). Strap-on sex has a lot to do with suspension of disbelief; a well-fitting, comfortable harness

→

that holds your dildo (or, if you prefer, your "dick") firmly in place will help with that. Because nothing kills a "Who's your daddy?" moment like a mandatory time-out as a result of malfunctioning equipment.

Basic strap-on harnesses come in two styles: single strap or two strap (see illustration, page 95). A single-strap harness fits exactly like a G-string and is therefore pretty impractical for men, because, duh, there's already a nonsilicone willy in the way. Women, though, have no preexisting package to worry about and might actually enjoy the additional clit stimulation a single-strap harness provides. A single-strap exception for men is BL's Man's Harness ($$$$)—you'll recognize it by the hanging "codpiece" designed to hold his original equipment. And, yes, sometimes men like to strap one on, too: Maybe he wants to keep going after he's, uh, petered out, or perhaps his girlfriend gets a huge crush on a supersize purple dildo at her local sex-toy shop—not the kind of thing she'd want to face every night,

but once a year on her birthday, why not? A two-strap harness, on the other hand, fits exactly like a jock strap, making it perfect for guys, not to mention a great alternative for women who can't stand the wedgie-like feeling of a thong. See also **Bend Over Beginner Kit** and *Bend Over Boyfriend*.

harnesses, face

Chin straps, head harnesses, and **ball gags** with O-rings allow you to strap a dildo onto your face, so you look like a XXX unicorn or a stem-cell scientist's research project

→

gone horribly, *horribly* wrong. For obvious reasons, they're usually named something like the Humiliator. You'll find a few at EB ($$$) and EX ($$).

harnesses, fitting

Most harnesses are one size fits all, though a few offer size options. The black **patent leather** Black Cat harness (BL, $$$) is particularly good for thin lizzies. Adjust your harness (using the buckles or D-rings) until it is comfortably snug—the snugger the fit, the more control the wearer has over the **silicone** dong, and the more clitoral stimulation she will get from the base of the dildo. Buckles won't loosen during the sesh, which sometimes happens with D-rings. But the corollary to that is that D-rings allow the wearer to easily adjust the harness mid-sesh—especially handy for beginners still getting used to the fit of their setup.

harnesses, fixin's for

You'll need to make sure your harness works with your **dildo(s)** of choice (speaking of: see **receiver's choice**). For extra-small (aww!) or extra-large (eek!) dildos, you'll probably need a harness that comes with an adjustable O-ring, like those in the Terra Firma range (BL, GV, LB, WT; $$-$$$, depending on material). The O-ring is the part where the dildo pokes through. If the ring is too small, you might break your dildo (double eek!), and if the ring is too large, you'll be stuck with a wobbly dildo—*terribly* embarrassing, not to mention pretty useless. Or, worse, the dildo could slip right out of your harness, leaving you feeling all emasculated and your partner feeling all abandoned with a dildo sticking out of their bottom (turkey's done!). For more average pokers, most any harness will work—harnesses with fixed-size O-rings are all $1\frac{3}{4}$ inches in diameter.

Just be sure to test your dildo with the harness before you buy. If you're dead set on a certain harness but find it is too big for your favorite slim-jim dildo, ask a sales assistant if they stock foam rings (called Slip Nots at GV; $) to help you correct the problem. Finally, some harnesses are fitted with a pad that sits on the mons behind the O-ring; others are built with an open O-ring, so that the dildo presses directly against your skin. The wearer might prefer the stimulation of direct skin contact; alternatively, she might find that the pad prevents her pubes from getting caught in the contraption (yowza!). Open O-rings also allow for double dildos (see **dildos, double**), in case you like to get while you give.

harnesses, materials for

Once you've settled on the style that's right for you, you'll need to pick a material. Nylon is perfect for a first harness (and, if you ask us, a second, and a third . . .): The nylon Terra Firma is affordable ($$ at BL), it's non-scary looking (the straps look and work just like back-pack straps), and it's machine washable. And, hey, that last feature means you can take it in the shower!

If nylon isn't hardcore enough for you, there's always **leather**—the Terra Firma comes in cowhide, too. It's more expensive ($$$) and way harder to get clean, because you can't soak it—you have to just wipe it clean with a soapy cloth. **Patent leather**, however, is easier to clean—and so shiny, too! You can try the Corset Harness, by Sportsheets (available on EX, $$$); it's got garter straps and a lace-up back that makes your butt look like a heart. Kinky **vegans** can opt for rubber instead—it's got all the fetish cred of leather, and it's waterproof, too! Then there's **vinyl**, which is a nice mix of deviant-lite (like leather and rubber, it usually comes with buckles rather than D-rings) and practi-

→

cal (the material is sturdy and long lasting). The Peek-a-Boo harness (cheapest at BF, $$) is actually made of totally *clear* vinyl—perfect for those days when you've just trimmed your pubes into a heart shape and/or decorated them with jewels, and just can't bear to cover them up. (Though we can't imagine that it stays too clean and pristine for long.)

in nylon or $$$ in **leather**) lets you take advantage of all those squats at the gym—you can even wear one each and screw in the scissors position for an all-around **silicone** sesh. BF sells a slightly less sexy neoprene thigh harness that looks like a knee brace ($). Thigh harnesses also leave your genitals open to anything—particularly handy if you've got a pinch hitter in town. Or you could try the **Night Rider harness** (BL; $$), which can be attached to *anything*.

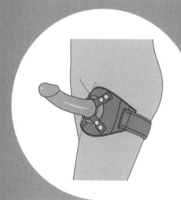

harnesses, thigh

Who says you have to strap one on in the same place every single time—that's so bourgeois! BL's Thigh One On harness ($$

harnesses, vibrating

Looking for a little extra for the missus? Many harnesses contain handy pockets designed to fit a **miniature vibrator** so the lady can get a little clitoral stimulation when she straps one on. BL's **leather** Buzz Me Tender harness (single-strap version is $$$, two-strap is a few dollars more) even has *two* pockets so the receiver can get a little vibe action, too. If your harness doesn't have a pocket,

H

you can always make it buzz by pairing it with a dildo that has a **bullet** vibe in its base—see **dildos, vibrating**.

headphones/ ear plugs

Ear plugs aren't just for construction workers and insomniacs, and noise-canceling headphones aren't just for prissy cubicle workers. Controlling your partner's soundtrack (or lack of one) takes **sensory deprivation** to a whole new level, especially when combined with a **blindfold**. If white noise is too nerdy for you, make a booty mix on your **iPod** and have your partner listen to it through headphones. Headphones and earplugs deprive your partner of aural clues and distractions, insulating them from sounds like your breathing, the smack of a **paddle** hitting their skin, the dog barking, etc. They can only speak when spoken to, and they can only be spoken to

when you choose to lean in real close and lift their headphones. This all helps your partner focus—exactly what that prissy cubicle worker is going for, too, except the object of focus in this case is not what's happening on a spreadsheet but, rather, what's happening on a bedsheet.

Hello Kitty vibrator

A long time ago in a galaxy far, far away—okay, so it was in Japan, and the year was 1997—this toy company called Genyo licensed the Hello Kitty brand to make a line of toys, one of which was a Hello Kitty vibrating shoulder massager. Of course, it didn't take long for people to figure out that the, ahem, shoulder massager could be used elsewhere. A few years later, the Hello Kitty (or Kitty-chan, as they say in Japan) "**vibrator**" became a regular fixture in Japanese adult videos. By 1999, the toy was for sale in vending machines in "love hotels" across the country (you know, the same vending machines that stock teen girls' soiled undies). Needless to say, Hello Kitty's peeps were pissed off, and a lengthy legal battle ensued, which finally ended only because Genyo was busted on tax fraud and the Hello Kitty team was able to swoop in and break the massager molds. Bye-bye, Kitty! (Unless, of course, you're comfortable bidding for a used vibrator on eBay . . .)

hemorrhoids

Hemorrhoids are swollen veins in the anal region caused by constipation (all that straining),

diarrhea (or "rushed jobs"), pregnancy, labor (again, all that straining), or obesity. They are decidedly not caused by **anal play**, **dildos**, **anal beads**, **butt plugs**, a reach-around pinkie, or any other activity encouraged in this encyclopedia, *at least if all these things are high quality, safe, and used or done correctly.* Sure, anal play might *irritate* preexisting hemorrhoids, or you might *discover* hemorrhoids right *after* an anal sesh—in which case you should see your doc for treatment, and you should probably lay off the anal until they're healed. But the idea that safe and informed anal play *causes* hemorrhoids is an urban myth spread by tightasses.

high-end sex toys

Some hoity-toity folks (or those aspiring to be hoity-toity) believe that if something is über-expensive and as sleek and chic as an iPod, it's okay to stick it down your pants. Hence the emerging product lines and store retailers catering to ladies who lunch and Diddy (or whatever the fuck he's calling himself today). The new designs are elegant, the **materials** are (usually) better for you, the quality is (usually) skyscraper high, and the price tags are what's truly obscene about the toys.

PVibe's self-titled patented penis **vibrator** (basically a posh vibrating cock **ring**) is small and silent; it comes in stainless steel ($130), silver ($200), and gold ($300). They also make a sleek and simple miniature **waterproof** Cigar vibe in the same materials (and in the same price range). JimmyJane.com's Little Somethings are pretty much the same cigarillo idea, only slightly bigger, and at about the same price—one of only a handful of innocuous designs.

Conceptual designer Shiri Zinn (shirizinn.com) makes a few erotic pieces, including the Minx (illustrated), a handcrafted pink vibrator decorated with Swarovski crystals and a detachable pink feather or

fur tail; it comes with a silver engraved stand and is packaged in a handcrafted snakeskin box with satin lining ($300). Mi-Su.com sells two **butt plugs** (one of obsidian, or volcanic glass, and one of rose quartz) for $700, a diamond cock **ring** for almost $1,000, and a $1,600 black obsidian **dildo** in the shape of a small, Dalíesque bowling pin. They will even work with you to create your very own custom Mi-Su Couture toy (your kids don't need to go to college, do they?). And don't forget the aeronautically inspired **Elemental Pleasures** wands ($200-$400) or the slightly less expensive mini **Lelo** vibes, from Sweden.

Then there are the fancy-schmancy retail stores that sell

H

many of these designers' items. *Newsweek* reported that when Myla (Myla.com), a London-based "sensuality boutique," opened a store in New York, it had a one-month waiting list for its almost-$400 handcrafted, black, rechargeable vibrator called Bone (as in skeletal, not phallic). On 5th Avenue, Rykiel Woman is Henri Bendel's third-floor den of expensive sin. And Kiki de Montparnasse (Kikidm.com) is New York City's latest destination for chic bed-side accessories. We're just waiting for the cheap knock-offs to show up on Canal Street.

Hitachi Magic Wand

Where to start? It's the Cadillac of vibrators, the Tom Cruise of turbo-toys, the best seller, the MVP, the **girl's best friend**, the box office sure thing, that sev-enties toy. The Hitachi is *the* most popular vibrating sex toy in the world. The world! Like the **Wahl vibrator**, the Hitachi is marketed as a muscle mas-sager. It makes sense—after all, electric body massagers work by bringing blood to the area, which is—hey!—exactly what happens when you get turned on. And because the Hitachi was designed to be a work-horse, it can last for decades—unlike those crappy **novelties** designed to last for the dura-tion of a **bachelorette party**.

The Hitachi is the toy that inspired Joani Blank to start **Good Vibrations**. Masturbation maven Betty Dodson started ordering them by the case in the seventies to give out to women taking her self-love classes. Sure, the Hitachi sounds like a dying cow, but once you feel its strong vibrations, you won't care about waking the neigh-bors. Just try *not* to have an orgasm when you hold one of these puppies against your **clitoris**—though you may need to temper its strong vibra-tions with jeans or a pillow in between. Or just squeeze it between your thighs and let the vibes travel north. The

H

Hitachi has a soft foam head covered in soft **vinyl**, about the size of a tennis ball, and a foot-long white plastic handle (so no arm cramps!). Sure, it's not as cute as the **Rabbit Habit**— in fact, it's rather medical looking. But if you've got a nosy housekeeper or a dog who likes to drag inappropriate "presents" into the living room whenever your mother-in-law is over for tea, that might be a good thing. The Hitachi is a plug-in device, and it's an outie **vibrator** only—but it can be turned into an innie toy with one of the specially designed attachments (see following). The Hitachi's head is **porous**, so no sharing. It can be **cleaned** with a damp soapy cloth. Remember, if it doesn't say Hitachi, it's a knock-off. Imported from Japan by **Vibratex** and available every-where; BF is cheapest ($$). See also **"back" massagers** and **Berman Center Intimate Accessories**.

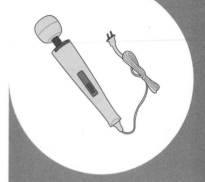

Hitachi Magic Wand attachments

The Cadillac of vibrators is an outie **vibrator** only—but it can be turned into an innie toy with one of the specially designed attachments. The **silicone** Gee-Whiz attachment, by VC ($$), fits over the head of the Hitachi to provide probing **G-spot** or **prostate** stimula-tion. Then there are a slew of **vinyl** attachments: The Wonder Wand fits over the Hitachi head for straight-up (literally) pene-tration ($), the vinyl **G-Spotter** (illustrated; also available in **rubber**) is shaped like the Gee-Whiz (BF, GV; $), the Deluxe →

G-Spotter has a stiffer, more solid protrusion (BF, BL; $), and the Magic Connection has a knob for attaching **Wahl vibrator** parts, which should *not* be used for penetration (BF; $). Finally, MP sells a **jelly** attachment that turns the Hitachi into a beaded insertable vibe ($). The attachments should be cleaned according to their respective **materials** and dressed up in a **condom** if you're sharing or if they're jelly or vinyl.

puke if it doesn't make you come first. It's 3 inches from head to toe, hiding a vibrating **bullet** within, with a long cord to the slide control. And the little arms raised over the pink cub's head, as if he were practicing for *The Nutcracker,* will flitter and flutter against your clit, nips, or anything else external. So wrong it's right. Takes two AA batteries; **monogamous** use only ($$ on BL, DS, MP; half the price on BF).

H

Honey Bear

A big **Vibratex** seller, this little bear of high-quality **vinyl** is so damn cute it might make you

Honey Dust, by Kama Sutra

See second definition of **massage oil, body.**

hysteria

What vibrators were born of. Back in the 1800s, hysteria (literally, "womb disease") was considered the most common "disorder" among women; its symptoms were mental and emotional distress, thought to be brought on by the womb's revolt against sexual deprivation. (Live in a sexist society where you can't vote or work and you have to submit to the uninspired jackhammering of your owner/husband, and you'd be distressed, too.) By some estimates, as many as three-quarters of all women suffered from this "hysteria," and, in fact, mention of the ailment can be found as early as 4 BC. The "cure" was a doctor-administered genital massage that would lead to "hysterical paroxysm"— in other words, an orgasm. Talk about bedside manner. Not surprisingly, these treatments never provided a permanent "cure"; rather, doctors found that their "frigid" female patients kept returning in droves for regular manual administrations.

Doctors who ran out of elbow grease would fob off the work to midwives.

Then, in 1869, an American doctor invented a steam-powered mechanical device to replace the manual genital massage— and, behold, the world's first **vibrator**! These devices became widespread (and, eventually, battery operated), and women continued to return from the doctor's office with flushed cheeks and secret smiles. Then, in the 1920s, the porn industry finally figured out what was going on, and these "medical devices" started making guest appearances in adult films. The secret was out! Kinda—it wasn't until 1952 that the American Psychiatric Association finally dropped the term *hysteria* from its books.

H

I

I Rub My Duckie

See **Duckie waterproof vibrator**.

ice

One end of the **temperature-play** continuum (hot **candle wax** being the other). Cheap, readily accessible, nonstaining, and just a teeny bit kinky, one cold cube—traced down someone's back on a hot summer's day, or strategically placed on a lazy nipple, or sucked on right before an oral administration—can make an otherwise ordinary sesh extra hot. Just be sure to keep the actual ice on the outside of the bod and away from delicate internal linings. See also **sensation** play and **DIY**.

ice cubes, aromatic

Jazz up your frosty play with some fragrant ice cubes, and stimulate two senses at once! (Yes, we were Home Shopping Network hosts in a former life.) Sephora.com sells "sensual rice steam-perfumed ice cubes" by Kenzoki. They're chemical free and full of essential oils, which must be why they cost about $30 for twelve cubes. ("*For ice?!*" we can hear our mothers asking.) The rice-plant ingredients cause the cubes to turn into a creamy, milky fluid as they melt—we guess that could be a good thing. For a cheaper **DIY** sensation accessory, make your own by freezing floral water, essences, infusions, etc.—all available at your local health food store or crunchy pharmacy—in an ice cube tray.

iPod

Yes, your iPod is a sex toy! Come on, a music mix that lasts longer than forty-five minutes, with no commercial breaks? That's the best thing to happen to sex since dimmer switches! (See **lighting**.) By the way, if your booty mix doesn't include either Muse or the Brazilian Girls, you're missing out.

Japanese sex toys

Ah, Japan: home of geishas, pornographic comics, pillow books, automated "love hotels," and sidewalk vending machines that dispense soiled schoolgirl undies. Is it any surprise that the famous **Rabbit Habit** hails from this country? The legendary toy is a sexy little loophole: A now-defunct Japanese law once prohibited the manufacture of sex toys that resembled genitalia, so Japanese vibrators featured rabbits, dolphins, beavers, fish, and funny cartoon faces. The law is now gone, but the dolphins and rabbits buzz on. (For a German version of disturbingly cute sex toys, see **Fun Factory**.) The Japanese porn industry, on the other hand, continues to be heavily regulated: A still-active law states that in moving animation or video, genitalia must

→

always be distorted by a blurred section called a "mosaic." *Now* do you understand why the Japanese came up with *bukkake?* (Google it if you dare.) Necessity might be the mother of invention, but repression is its naughty little friend. And don't even get us started on the complicated art of *shibari,* otherwise known as Japanese **rope** bondage ('cause, to be honest, we don't really know anything about it). See also **Hello Kitty vibrator**.

jelly rubber

Cheap plastic made with a **phthalate** softener. Jelly is highly flexible, usually translucent with lots of little bubbles, sticky to the touch, and stinky like a cheap shower-curtain liner—that's the unstable chemicals seeping out. Do you really want to stick that you-know-where? Some people report inflammation, burning, and a yeastlike discharge after using jelly toys, and recent studies suggest that exposure to phthalates may do serious (i.e., permanent) damage. Yes, you may be completely happy with your jelly **Nubby G**—*for now.* So, to be safe, slap a **condom** on before insertion. (You want explosive orgasms, not radioactive ones.) Use only water-based **lubes**, as others will actually melt the material. In fact, a jelly toy may break down simply from being in contact with a toy of another material. Expect some discoloration over the years, even if you're a clean freak. Some say to use mild soap or toy cleaner to wash it, while others say use no soap at all; everyone agrees you should avoid harsh dishwashing liquid or alcohol, which may also dissolve it. And make sure your jelly toy is air dried before storing it in a locked box by itself in the corner of a closet in your basement.

So, why are we even including any jelly toys in this book? Because they are everywhere: If you spy a sex toy, chances are it's jelly. Plus, because it's so malleable, it often makes for toys with really interesting textures that people love, and, because it's so cheap, it makes for very affordable toys (consider the endless array of jelly **sleeves**), so they become big sellers. But here's to putting our money where our twats are and making jelly toys tank in the market.

K

Kama Sutra bath & body products

The Bath & Body Works of the sex-toy industry. Kama Sutra makes affordably priced oils, creams, bath gels, and balms, most of which are edible and all of which are tastefully packaged. We like them so much, in fact, that we're raving about them despite them refusing to send free samples our way (how "Eastern" is that?). They specialize in gift baskets, and probably make a killing 'round Valentine's Day. More info at KamaSutra.com. See also **body paint**; **edible accessories**; and **massage oil, body**.

Kegelcisor

A stainless-steel vaginal barbell—pretty much the exact same thing as the **Betty's**

→

Barbell dildo (BL; $$$). See Kegelcisor.com for more info. See also **metals**.

kegels

Arnold Kegel, M.D., spent the middle of the last century studying urinary incontinence and sexual dysfunction in women and found that strong **pelvic floor muscles** (which include the PC muscle) are key to righting such wrongs. (These muscles contract involuntarily during orgasm and voluntarily when you've got to pee like a racehorse.) "Kegels" are the squeezing technique the good doctor developed to tone the pelvic floor and, today, there are several toys are made specifically with that workout in mind. Men can work on their kegels with the **Aneros**, while women can also choose among **Betty's Barbell dildo**, the **Kegelcisor**, the **Berman Center**'s Adonis, the **Lumina Wand**, and the new kid on the block that everyone's raving about, **Natural Contours**' Energie. All these toys come with

instructions for your pelvic workout. Double dildos (see **dildos, double**) like the **Feeldoe** and the **Nexus** will work, too. Or, for a prop-free routine, browse Kegel-Exercises.com or the "Pumping up Your Love Muscles" chapter of our first book, *The Big Bang*.

kits

Every sex-toy outlet sells its own kits, and they all make great gifts. The kit packaging is like a reassurance from on high that, yes, people give and receive sex toys all the time. *("You got an erection set for your birthday? Man, I want one of those!")* Plus, buying a kit typically means that you don't have to figure out what **lube** goes with your **dildo** or cock **ring**, etc., because everything you need is already in there. There are way too many kits for us to list them all, but we have yet to meet a kit we didn't like. What can we say? We're suckers for packaging. In particular, for **bath** time, we like GV's Friday Night Delight ($$). For covering all your bases, we like BL's Sex Toys 101 Kit ($$$; see **beginner toys**). For form *and* function, we like the **Mile-High Kit** ($$). And, for **anal play**, the final frontier, it's gotta be the **Bend Over Beginner Kit** ($$). See also **etiquette, gift-giving**.

kinky toys

Anything outside the main-stream, where *mainstream* means women's magazines, an episode of *Sex and the City,* a **bachelorette party**, a **Tupperware**-style sex-toys party, or the sex-toy section of DS. A kinky toy would not be referred to as a "marital aid" and is probably not the kind of toy your couples counselor would recommend. Also, a kinky toy is not the kind that would be featured in a slapstick comedy featuring a rascally dog that likes to go rummaging in guests' suitcases—a kinky toy is not a punch line. For example, a **Rabbit** is mainstream; a **gimp suit** is kinky. See also **BDSM**.

latex gloves

Latex gloves get a bad rap—mention them in the context of sex (as opposed to, say, doing the dishes or home-dyeing your hair), and most people will joke nervously about body-cavity searches, **prostate** exams, or having their legs up in stirrups. But, hey, some of the hottest sex fantasies begin their lives as nervous jokes, and what better accessory to these fantasies than a pair of **latex** gloves? Some fetish retailers even stock elbow-length gloves in multiple colors, if you're really serious about getting into character (EX; $$).

But latex gloves aren't just aesthetic props—they're handy for safer sex, too. Tiny invisible cuts on your hands can transmit **STDs**—both ways, and in both cavities. Besides, if you're tak-ing a whole hand *anywhere,* a well-lubed latex glove will ease your entry. (Just put "hangnail" and "delicate anal tissue" in

→

the same sentence and you'll know *exactly* what we're talking about.) But even if you're not going in whole-handedly, barrier protection is a pretty good idea. (Yeah, yeah, we know you're not going to do it, but it's our duty to mention it anyway.) Sure, fingering is safer than fucking, but jumping off a two-story building is safer than leaping off a skyscraper, too, you know. For vaginal fantasies, you should avoid powdered gloves, since talc has been linked to cervical cancer (or just thoroughly rinse off the powder first). Some people like to make **dental dams** out of latex gloves by cutting off the four fingers, slitting up the side opposite the thumb, rinsing off the powder, and lubing up—but that seems like an awful lot of work when a piece of sturdy **Saran Wrap** does the job just fine. (There are also purpose-made Sheer Glyde dental dams.)

But wait—there's more! Wearing latex gloves when you're knocking on someone's back door means you won't have to stop and wash up before going anywhere else—a vagina, say. (You'll give the vagina owner one mother of a urinary-tract infection if you don't wash up or use gloves between orifices.) You can simply change or remove the glove and keep on trucking—no buzz-killing trip to the bathroom required. For all uses, you should avoid oil-based **lubes**, as oil can degrade latex. Stick to water- or silicone-based lubes, unless you're using polyurethane gloves (if your partner has a latex allergy, say), in which case any lube will do. *"Okay, Mr. Ben Dover, the doctor will see you now."*

latex rubber

As found in nature, latex is the milky-white juice of many plants, most commonly the rubber tree, which can be made into natural latex rubber. But latex can be made synthetically and then turned into rubber, too. It's inexpensive (probably the most inexpensive toy material besides a cucumber), it can be sculpted into most any shape, size, and color (though flesh tone and black are the most common), and, though it's firmer and less smelly than jelly, it will wear out faster.

Latex is **porous**, so you should use a latex condom with your latex toys (isn't it ironic?). It's not porous enough to make **condoms**, **latex gloves**, and **dental dams** ineffective—unlike very porous animal-skin condoms. Never use oil-based **lubes**, because they'll break down the latex; water- and silicone-based lubes are a-okay. Alcohol will also break it down, so, instead, clean it with a soapy cloth. Keep in a cool, dry place.

Allergies to latex were first recognized in the late seventies and have been on the rise with the increase of the material in the environment. Caused by a protein in *natural* latex rubber, allergies can develop over time the more you are exposed to the material. (Though synthetic latex is not an allergen, most products that mention latex mean the natural kind, and there's usually no way of knowing for sure—so, if you're allergic,

avoid *anything* with *latex* on the label). If you start experiencing inflammation, a rash, or discharge after using latex, it's time to switch to **silicone** toys and polyurethane **condoms**. A note to the allergic: In addition to testing all their toys for **phthalates**, **A-Womans-Touch.com** has a chemist check all their toys for latex, so, if they say something is latex free, you know you can trust 'em. An example of a latex **dildo** is Mr. Realistic (MP; $$$).

Laya Spot vibrator

This petite external **vibrator** is one of those **contour toys**—chic, ergonomic, and designed to follow the curves of a woman's body. It's a tad smaller than a computer mouse (4¼ inches by 1½ inches), which means it can sit inside your cupped hand, lie on your pubic bone, or sit between your thighs, giving you a more intimate experience than some of the bulkier vibes out there. The Laya's perfect for →

women who like a little labia attention; hold it down a little farther for a nice **perineum** massage. Guys might like it cupped around their balls, too. Controlled with two light-up, soft-touch buttons, it's got eight speeds of constant vibration and three of pulsing vibration, from barely there to pretty intense. It's no **Hitachi**, but its vibrations are nevertheless pretty fierce for a small AAA battery-operated toy. And quiet! Laya's manufactured by **Fun Factory**, so you know it's built to last: It's made of their Elastomed, a hard, **nonporous**, hypoallergenic **elastomer**. Just wash with soap and water. A packet of lube is included ($$). See also **Lelo vibrators** and **Pure Bliss vibrator**.

Le Lynx vibrator

See **ElementalPleasures.com.**

leather

Treated cow flesh. Doesn't sound so sexy when we—okay, when Lo—puts it like that, huh? And yet people, especially the **BDSM** and gay-biker communities, embrace it as the ultimate sex **material**. Dildo **harnesses** are often made of leather, but why? It can't be disinfected or boiled or even cleaned very well, so body fluids sink into it, like, *forever.* You could try using leather cleaners and saddle soaps. But for safety and sanitary reasons, you might want to go with machine-washable nylon, which is better for the environment than **rubber**, **vinyl**, and, yes, leather. Be free, Bessie, be free! If you simply *must* add a little leather to your collection, do it with something that's not likely to get soiled, like a **bondage belt**.

Lelo vibrators

Did you ever find a smooth piece of sea glass on the beach and keep it in your pocket because it felt so nice to hold in your hand and rub with your thumb? A Lelo "pleasure object" is like that, only you hold it in your hand and rub it against your clitoris. This **high-end sex toy** company based in Sweden makes several versions of its elfin pebble vibe (3½ inches by 2 inches): the Lily vibrator ("pearly" nonporous **elastomer**; around $130), the Nea (porcelain-like with a floral motif; just under $100), the Ida (shiny, water-proof rubber, with lips that hug the clitoris; around $170), and the Yva (medical-grade surgical steel; around $1,300—*or* 18K gold plate; about $1,500).

They're basically the spoiled little sisters of the **Laya Spot vibrator** (though they're not officially related—more like BFFs): external, ergonomic, **contour toys** that can be set on or around the **clitoris**, curved around the vulva/balls, or pressed against the **perineum**.

You could even use one as a nipple teaser. And, because they're so small, you can easily and comfortably incorporate them into intercourse or oral. Still feeling gypped by their high-end price tags? Unlike the Laya, the Lelos are rechargeable—just plug them in like you would a cell phone! When fully charged, they can go for seven hours, and they have a 90-day stand-by time. All Lelo toys come in a gift box with a satin **storage** pouch, are quieter than a mouse, feature LED indicators, and have a one-year warranty. The most popular and affordable, the Lily vibe, is available on BL, BF, LB, and MP; they're all available on Lelo.com. See also **Pure Bliss vibrator**.

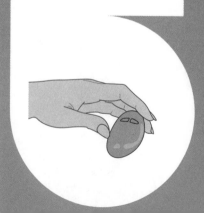

Libida.com (LB)

The only online retail site designed especially for straight women, Libida.com features not just toys but also an erotic gallery, erotic literature, two staff sexologists, a sexual-health library, advice, and even weekly sexual horoscopes (*so girly!*). Their "Decision Maker" guides newbies through an easy step-by-step process to finding the perfect toy. But what really sets them apart: a Libida Meter that rates toys (on vibe intensity, volume, versatility, and clitoral/anal/G-spot friendliness) and DVDs (on explicitness, romance, cinematography, acting, plot, men's appeal, chemistry, women's pleasure, taboos, and racial diversity). Unfortunately, the Libida Meter gave the **Pocket Rocket vibrator** three out of five stars for being **G-spot** and anal friendly. Huh? We wouldn't stick that toy inside *anywhere*, especially not the butt! Plus, their site design is just not that inviting, and their collection is limited. Well, nobody's perfect—especially in the sex-toy industry, where there are no industry standards. Except when it comes to prices—and theirs are. Industry standard, we mean.

lighting

Sometimes **candles** are a little too Harlequin Romance or Colonial Williamsburg—and that doesn't work for every kind of sex. But overhead fluorescent lighting doesn't work for *any* kind of sex (except for maybe that sexy-gynecologist role-playing scenario you've been working on). For times like these, have some 15-watt bulbs on hand, or install a dimmer switch in the bedroom. You can buy a kit at the hardware store, and it's a cinch to install—we swear. Cheap, too! Bulb: $1. Dimmer kit: $7. Not worrying about whether your lover is distracted by your ass pimples: priceless.

Lily vibrator

See **Lelo vibrators**.

lipstick vibe

See **undercover toys**.

liquid latex

See **body paint**.

Little Flirt butt plug

TantusSilicone.com's Little Flirt is just about the smallest, cutest **butt plug** you'll ever meet (3 inches by 7/8 inches). As long as you use enough water-based **lube**, a wee butt plug like this should be able to slip in the back without much fuss—see **anal play** and **butt plugs** for more tips on how to make your rear entrance. Made of **silicone**, so boil or wash and use with a water-based **lube**. Available everywhere (WT calls it Petunia) for about ten bucks.

lubes or lubricants, about

If you don't think of friction relievers as sex toys, you're not using them right. If you always assumed that lube was just a postmenopause substitute for the real thing, or a prison guard's tool of the trade for a kinder, gentler body-cavity search, you've been seriously missing out. Like parsley, lube is the ideal garnish for any dish. First off, you shouldn't be going anywhere *near* the anus without a little lube, not even with a smaller-than-average pinkie—there's zero natural lubrication back there, and spit just won't cut it. Next, *all* handwork feels

→

better with a little lube. On him, lube means you can pump his pole harder and faster without giving him rug burn. On her, lube means she can take more, and more varied, stimulation all over, without getting chafed or oversensitive (her little man in the boat is particularly delicate).

During oral, you might enjoy the addition of a little lube (may we interest you in a flavor?) to help you slide around, especially if you're hungover and suffering from a serious case of dry mouth. Or, next time you're going down on your partner, just put a little lube on your finger and let it wander to the **perineum** or the starfish (just don't let it wander back to the front). Finally, even old-school penis-in-vagina sex can be improved by lube, especially during a quickie (when there's no foreplay buildup) or a marathon sesh. Adding lube to a **condom** means it's less likely to break, and adding a drop of lube *inside* a condom will improve his **latex** experience, too. A woman's natural lube should not be considered a measuring stick for how into it she is—some women gush at the brush of an elbow, while others produce only a drop or two during the best sex of their life. Plus, dehydration, the time of the month, medications, age, and a hangover are just a few factors that may diminish her own geyser. Lube: It does a body good.

Most sex-toy shops offer lube sampler packs or trial-size sachets. **Blowfish** sells a water-based lube sampler and a silicone sampler ($$ each), both of which include most of the lubes we review here. Once you've settled on a favorite—or a few favorites—you can invest in a full bottle with a pump dispenser (put it in a cup of warm water to avoid the shock of freezing-cold liquid on your nuts). The dispenser allows for one-handed reapplication (which means that reapplication is less likely to disrupt the flow of events). If, however, you're in a casual-dating phase and are entertaining a steady stream of luvvers, you might want to steer clear of those industrial-size vats of lube—it's a little off-putting, especially when there's only half an inch left in the bottom. Save the economy shopping for your LTRs.

You have a number of lube options, depending on the body part or toy, the body cavity, the condom, and the conditions (can you say "hot tub"?). The three basic lube food groups are oil based, silicone based, and water based. For lube reviews by category, see **lubes, oil-based**; **lubes, silicone-based**; and **lubes, water-based** following. If you've been contemplating just using a handy household product instead, please see **lubes, DIY** first.

None of the lubes we recommend contain **Nonoxynol-9**. And please note: Some lubes, especially flavored lubes, contain a natural sugar called glycerin (for sweetness), which can be irritating to oversensitive vaginas, sometimes causing a yeast infection (not so sweet). So, if you're not working with a vagina of steel, steer clear of any lubes containing glycerin.

lubes, DIY

DIY lubes are for hand-jobs-for-him only: The vagina is too prone to infection (bless its sensitive little lining), and most do-it-yourself lubes tend to be oil based, which means they're not **latex** compatible. But if a hand job is all that's on the menu (i.e., you're sure it won't escalate to something requiring a **condom** or a vagina), you might want to try cheap hand lotion like Vaseline Intensive Care (the more expensive stuff absorbs too well), olive oil, Crisco, baby oil, hair conditioner if you're in the shower (shampoo is too drying), and Kiss My Face Moisture Shave mixed with one part water (five bucks at DS—just try it). Spit can feel good and raunchy, but it doesn't last long, and cotton mouth will set in almost immediately.

lubes, oil-based

Oil-based lubes can't be used with latex products (condoms, dams, diaphragms), and they're not particularly compatible with vaginas, either. Oil has a tendency to hang around, which makes it a very hardy lube, but a very likely culprit in urinary-tract infections in women, too. (If you must know, it's because UTIs are caused by microscopic fecal bacteria, and, during a particular athletic sesh, even just penis-in-vagina sex, that bacteria gets bumped around. It's why women prone to infection should always pee right after sex: It clears the tract. But oil can't be peed away easily; it just hangs around, keeping the bacteria company. And lube gets everywhere, so even if you're using it in the back door, it's gonna travel around to the front.)

So, the only oil-appropriate occasions are a) anal sex with a polyurethane condom, b) a man hand job that's not going to end up in vaginal sex, c) anal fisting (yowza!), or d) unprotected anal sex between two men (double yowza! Need we remind you that unprotected anal sex is the highest-risk sexual activity out there for STDs and HIV?).

Oil-based lubes are mostly household products like baby oil and Crisco—see lubes, DIY—or products designed specifically for manhandling. The latter can be easily spotted by their oh-so-manly names like Elbow Grease (comes in a one-gallon plastic bucket with handle; $$$ at CheapLubes.com), Boy Butter (made of vegetable oil; $ for 16 ounces at BF), Men's Cream (petroleum based; $ for 4 ounces at BF), Rocket Balm (tingly peppermint oil; $ for 1 ounce at GV), and the practically-dripping-with-testosterone-named Stroke 29 by Gun Oil (almond and coconut oil; $$ for 6 ounces at BL). For a latex-friendly manhandling product, see Eros Power Cream in lubes, silicone-based—$$ for 5 ounces at GV.

lubes, silicone-based

The future of sex is silicone, and the future of sex is now. (And, no, this has nothing to do with fake ta-tas.) Silicone lube feels and works just like oil—i.e., it's waterproof (bring on the shower nozzle!), a little goes a long way, and it's longer lasting than water-based lubes because it doesn't absorb into the body. But, *unlike* oil, it's safe to use on latex **condoms** and **dams** (bring on the hardcore anal fucking!). It's the only inert lube out there, meaning it won't react at all with your own body's chemistry—though if a silicone lube contains additives, as Pink does, it's no longer considered inert. You can even shave with it (to help keep the razor sharper longer).

There's one very important rule about silicone lubes, however: *Do not use silicone lubes on toys made from silicone or* **Cyberskin** *et al.* Because the only thing silicone bonds to is silicone, a weird chemical reaction occurs between silicone or Cyberskin toys and silicone lubes, causing the surface of the toys to get gummy (not really something you want going on *inside* you). However, there is an exception to this rule. As

silicone queen and **Tantus** president Metis Black told us, it all depends on the grade of silicone involved: If the toy is made from medical-grade platinum silicone (like all Tantus dildos) and the lube's ingredients contain dimethicone (first), dimethiconal, and cyclomenthicone (and no unnecessary additives like aloe or vitamin E), like with Eros Gel and Eros Original Bodyglide, then it should be perfectly safe.

But since it's hard to know exactly what's in a toy, you should *always* do a small patch test on the base of your toy first: If the lube stays slippery, you can keep on sliding. Even if you prefer to slap a **latex** condom on the toy just to be safe, you're still going to need to wash the silicone lube off *you* with soap and water, because it doesn't wash away as easily as water-based lube. (That's why it works in the hot tub, remember?)

"But what about the horror health stories of silicone seepage from burst breast implants?" you ask. Have no fear; silicone *lubes* are safe: They don't get absorbed by the epidermis of your body, which includes the lining of your body cavities.

Here are a few of our favorite silicone-based lubes (sensitive vaginas should avoid the products that contain glycerin). They're available all over, and most are about $10 for a 30-milliliter bottle. Silicone lubes tend to be more expensive than the water-based kind, but you need less, so it evens out.

And so, without further ado: Eros Gel or Eros Original Bodyglide (glycerin free and safe to use with Tantus silicone dildos); Eros Power Cream (contains glycerin); Wet Platinum (glycerin free); and Pink (best suited for her veegee, Pink comes in an elegant, hand-blown Italian glass jar, meaning it could easily pass for a chic bottle of perfume; glycerin free, though its additives—vitamin E and aloe vera—make it impossible to use with high-quality pure silicone dildos, so don't bother with the patch test).

lubes, water-based

Water-based lubes are great team players: You can use them with any toy, you can use them with latex **condoms** or **dams** (and diaphragms, for that matter), and they wash off easily with water. They are not waterproof, however, so if you need a lube for the hot tub, you should check out **lubes, silicone-based**. And beware of so-called water-*soluble* lubes, which frequently contain oil (and thus are not **latex** compatible). Here are a few of our favorite water-based lubes (sensitive vaginas should avoid the products that contain glycerin). They're available all over ($).

Astroglide: Fans claim it's the most natural-feeling lube out there; plus, they love its sweet taste. Detractors say it's so thin that it slides all over the place. Contains glycerin.

Liquid Silk: The perfect My First Lube—glycerin free, light, and nonsticky. The taste isn't great, so we'd steer clear of this one if you've got oral in mind.

Maximus: Very long lasting for a water-based lube, so a popular pick for anal activities. Taste free, odor free, glycerin free.

Probe Classic: Probe's Classic formula is the thickest water-based lube out there, and thus a favorite among backdoor friends. Probe's Silky Light formula is better suited to handwork and old-school intercourse. Taste free, odor free. Both contain glycerin.

Sensua Personal Lubricants: Chemical free, homeopathic, **vegan**, all-natural, available in peach or raspberry flavors, and glycerin free.

Sensual Power Lube: Glycerin free.

Slippery Stuff: Taste free, odor free, glycerin free.

can't pick just one). Maybe you don't like the taste of genitalia. Or perhaps you're one of those rare upstanding citizens who actually–*gasp*–uses barrier protection for casual encounters of the oral kind, in which case these lubes can jazz up the flavor of **latex**. It's better than grabbing something random from your fridge–chances are that'll either contain oil, which will destroy the latex, or sugar, which may give her a yeast infection (or, worse, both). As a bonus feature, Wet lubes come in an easy-grip contoured bottle, which will sound much more impressive if you've ever tried to open a tube of lube with a greasy hand. Wet Flavored Lubes are all surprisingly glycerin free.

lubes, water-based, flavored

For a plethora of flavors, from passion fruit to piña colada, the Wet water-based range is your friend (try a sampler pack if you

lubes, water-based, warming

In high school, Lo made a pilgrimage to the Pink Pussycat Boutique in NYC to get a

→

Valentine's Day present for her boyfriend and came back with a cheap bottle of Emotion Lotion that got hot when you rubbed it and tasted like strawberries (actually, it tasted like shit). Fifteen years later, K-Y comes out with a warming liquid (containing glycerin), and suddenly it's big news? Guess so, 'cause even your grandmother's heard of the new K-Y. The benefit of K-Y's brand is that it's available freakin' everywhere. The ladies at **Good Vibrations** prefer the water-based ID Warming Liquid, though it does contain glycerin, too. For a glycerin-free warming experience, there's Sliquid Sizzle. Some ladies swear by these muff warmers, while others claim it's all gimmick—make up your own mind. Try mixing your warming lube with a regular water-based lube for a more pleasingly slippery effect. These warming lubes, all water based, are not to be confused with genital warming massage oils—see **massage oils, genital**.

Lucite

A common brand name for hard **acrylic**. See also **materials**.

Lumina Wand

This hard **acrylic**, pretty-in-pink magic wand is one of those sex toys that could pass as abstract art—but, unlike many of those toys, it's more than just a pretty face. Two orbs at the base make for a firm, easy-to-grip handle, and the curve is specially formulated for easy G-spotting. Or, flip it around and use the knobby end in the vagina or ass for a pleasantly ridged approach to penetration. (Though the wand doesn't have a flared base, it's long enough—9 inches by 1¼ inches—that every retailer seems to consider it safe for **anal play**. Just don't let go of the knobby handle, and don't try to get all 9 inches in there, either.)

It's got no seams, which means it's silky smooth, and it's shatter resistant, too (as long as you don't keep dropping it on the ground over and over again to "test" it, as we did). And did we mention it comes with a black pleather carrying case? (Doesn't really go with the pink, but **vegetarians** will like it.) The Wand is **waterproof**, compatible with any kind of **lube**, **nonporous**, and can be washed with soap and water. Manufactured in China, it's distributed in the United States by BL ($$) and is also available at BF (as the G-spot Bloop Wand), DS (as the Crystal Wave), GV (as the Jupiter Dildo), LB (as the Crystal G), and MP (as Dangerous Curves). Yep, it's just that pretty that none of them could resist giving it their own special name.

M

massage oil, body

If you're new to sex toys, this is one of the best sex accessories to start with: affordable, sensual rather than shocking, and readily available. Oils are incompatible with **latex**, and not great on coochies either, so, for the "special" portion of your massage, you should switch to a specially formulated genital massage oil (see following). But for the body, any kind of oil will do.

At beauty outlets like the Body Shop (BodyShop.com) or Aveda (Aveda.com), you can buy plain oil (e.g., organic soy oil) and flavor it with your own favorite essential oil. For a flavored oil you can actually nibble on, try something from GV's Body Candy range (see **edible accessories**)—these surprisingly unsticky potions are made from a sweet almond-oil base. Body Butter (a GV exclusive; $), which comes in mint julep or raspberry-chocolate truffle, is a similar (edible) idea, except it comes in solid balm form and rubs in more like a moisturizing lotion than an oil. None of these oil-based products is latex or coochie compatible, but they *are* compatible with **vegetarians** (they contain no animal by-products).

A favorite among massage therapists (not to mention Betty Dodson) is Charlie Sunshine's Secret Formula Massage Oil (DS; $). It looks and feels like lotion (i.e., it's not going to slop all over your sheets like regular oil), but it's actually oil (so you won't need to reapply every ten seconds, as with some moisturizing lotions). It's made of all-natural products and contains lots of Vitamin E, which is good for the skin. For something very similar, try GV's own Massage Lotion, available in Sugar Plum, Venus (whatever the hell that planet smells like), and unscented ($ for 4 ounces). Finally, our three favorite body-massage gimmicks: ❶ GV's Massage Bar ($) looks like a

bar of soap, but it's actually a body-heat-activated massage oil made from cocoa butter and peppermint. You just rub it between your hands and you're good to go (which, "handily," warms the oil, too). This bar is neither latex nor coochie compatible. ❷ **Kama Sutra Honey Dust** ($ for 8 ounces at BF) is a sweet, edible body powder that comes with a feather applicator. We know, we know, a light dusting of shimmering gold isn't exactly a full-body massage, but if you're a lazy sensualist, this might come in handy every now and then. ❸ Massage candles whose warm wax turns into massage oil like magic. For details, see **candle wax**.

massage oil, genital

You want to avoid getting any kind of oil inside her cooch—either via internal massage or via oil on your penis that ends up giving her a very different kind of internal massage. Oil

→

has a tendency to hang around, which makes it a great massage lotion—and an even better host to all sorts of microscopic bacteria that can lead to veegee infections. Some ladies are never affected by this (in fact, we know one woman who's been masturbating with olive oil for years—*so* European), but is it worth the risk? Because nothing says "thanks for the erotic massage" quite like a piss-burning urinary-tract infection. So, keep your slaked snake out of there, and use the following products for *external* genital massage only. Afterward, make sure you pee and shower to remove all the oil and keep things kosher down there.

If you *really* want to heat things up, try an edible warming oil or a tingling menthol balm.

Warming oils and gels heat up as you blow on them (neato!). Motion Lotion (different from *Emotion* Lotion) comes in twelve fruity flavors—buy a sampler pack (GV; $) and try 'em all! Wet and Midnight Fire are two other brands—same idea, same cheesy naming strategy. We like **Kama Sutra** Oil of Love (BF; $ for 4 ounces) for its fairly classy packaging; it comes in cinnamon, vanilla, or plain. These warming oils are all latex friendly and edible, though edible and tasty are usually two entirely different concepts in this industry. None of them should be used internally (see the **lubes** section for that) or over the entire body, either.

Menthol balms are the same basic deal, except they're cool and tingly instead of warm and tingly. Try Flower Balm for her, peppermint Rocket Balm for him ($ at GV), or Kama Sutra Pleasure Balm (unisex; $ at BF). These balms are all edible, they are all for external, erogenous-zone use only, and *they are not latex compatible.*

masturbation sleeves

If you left an eighth-grade science geek-slash-chronic masturbator alone for long enough, eventually he'd come

→

M

up with a masturbation sleeve. In fact, most sleeves sound like they were named by horny *sixth*-grade science geeks: the **Fleshlight** (the best seller of the bunch), the Ecsta-Sleeve (GV's exclusive sleeve, so you know it's good), the Dream Sleeve (a better choice than the Fleshlight, in our humble opinion), the Erotic Embrace (smaller and cheaper, for travel), the Tunnel of Love, the Pocket Gal, Alexa's Vibrating Pussy, and our favorite, at least in corny concept, the Cheri. (The Cheri actually comes with a thin vinyl "hymen" for that special first-time feeling.) A masturbation sleeve is meant to simulate the feel of a vagina, mouth, or anus. The inside is typically made of either porous **jelly rubber** (if it's a bargain-basement model) or, more commonly, one of the new, **porous**, lifelike materials such as **Cyberskin**. Whatever's inside, the only way to *really* keep it clean is to wear a **condom**—or, in a pinch, you can wash it out with antibacterial soap and water and dry it with a little cornstarch.

Some vibrate, some have stimulating beads, some have ridges, and some have all three. One *could* consider this technological advancement to be a step backward for humankind, the way some believe video games distract from beneficial reading for fun. After all, think how a young man's imagination used to be pushed to its limits as he retooled everyday household objects into masturbation devices: a Ziploc-ed baggie of warm oatmeal shoved between two mattresses, a silky scarf pushed into a lump of foam, a duct-taped banana skin, or—if the boy was a Philip Roth fan—a cored apple or a baseball mitt. But, hey, if the Fleshlight prevents just one apple pie from being defiled before dinner, it will all have been worthwhile.

Guys willing to seriously invest in their wank habit can fork over a couple hundred bucks for toys like the Ultra-Realistic Vibrating Pussy and Anus (XA has a selection). These are basically sleeves in context and are often molded after **porn stars**—you get all the

M

naughty bits of the **RealDoll** without paying for those unnecessary limbs. Some people refer to masturbation sleeves as cock or penis **sleeves**, while others say "cock sleeve" actually means penis **extender**. People, can't we all get along? Sleeves are available just about everywhere for $$. See also **pumps, penis** and **porn-star toys.**

materials

It's amazing what we'll put in our bodies. Do you read the ingredient labels on everything you eat? And, if you did, would you know what half that stuff was? As consumers, we're responsible for educating ourselves about what we stick in our pie holes, baby holes, and bung holes—'cause the manufacturers just trying to make a buck sure aren't going to inform us. Fortunately, though, with more and more informed consumers making better choices, there's a growing consciousness about making toys that are good for the environment (which includes your bod). Since people use these toys on very intimate parts, especially in areas such as the vagina and the anal canal, where the skin is delicate and highly absorptive, it is important to use safe products: ones that work with your anatomy (one size doesn't always fit all), that won't cause abrasions to your most sensitive flesh (for instance, from rough seams), and that won't result in physical reactions to its chemicals (though some people are more sensitive or allergic than others).

Toys made of inferior materials are usually sticky, are impossible to clean, and/or carry a very strong odor. This odor is a result of a chemical reaction called outgassing (the release of vapors) caused by **phthalates** in **jelly rubber,** unstable **vinyl** (a.k.a PVC), and other soft plastics. That doesn't mean you *can't* use them; just use them with a **condom** (hey, it makes cleaning your toy a cinch). Admittedly, that can be tough, especially when the interesting texture of porous toys is probably what you

→

bought it for in the first place. A harder plastic like **acrylic** or **silicone** is a much safer, **nonporous** option, however.

But maybe you don't know what a toy is made of. If, after you use a sex toy, you're red or swollen or you feel "not right," chances are it was crap material. Even popular brand items that seem like a great idea may be poorly executed in terms of materials and design. And often either the materials aren't labeled on the packaging or the labels are misleading (i.e., they call it silicone when it's only *partly* made of silicone). There are no industry standards about what materials go into making a sex toy, or even about what those materials are called, so it's often impossible to know for sure. When in doubt with a mystery material, use a condom (with water- or silicone-based lube); if you just gotta ride bareback, though, stick with a water-based lube and dedicate the toy to just one person, 'cause it's probably **porous** (i.e., no matter how well you wash it with soap or a toy cleaner, you'll be swapping bacteria via the toy's pores). Basically, if you open a package and feel like you need a gas mask, some duct tape to hold it together, or anesthesia to keep from hurting yourself, stick with your gut instinct and don't stick it in anywhere.

For more specific details on the various materials toys are made of, see the entries for the bolded words in this entry, as well as **acrylic**; **Cyberskin**; **elastomer**; **glass**; **latex rubber**; **leather**; **metals**; **plastic, hard**; and **silicone**. See also **cleaning & care** and **storage**, and the Safety Tips Appendix.

metals

Chrome, brass, titanium, aluminum, stainless or surgical steel, silver, gold—sex toys can be made out of any of them. (Stainless steel may be the most environmentally conscious but may cause reactions in people allergic to nickel.) Like **glass**, metal insertables are **nonporous**,

phthalate free, firm on the **G-** and **P-spots**, super-slick with any kind of **lube**, and handy at transmitting heat and cold (just don't freeze it, lest you end up in an **X-rated** version of that scene from *A Christmas Story*). Go for solid metals rather than cheap metal coatings, which may flake off—*inside you.* Check for burrs as soon as you get a new metal toy anyway, just to be safe, and wash it before use (industrial manufacturing techniques to lathe a toy don't do a body good). If you can't wear anything but solid gold earrings, only use elemental metals (like titanium, niobium, etc.).

Cleanup varies, depending on the toy's construction and quality. For instance, though a cheap metal-coated toy might easily corrode if immersed in water, a **high-end** vibe from **Elemental Pleasures** can be put in the dishwasher—or the hot tub, for that matter. Thoroughly dry your metal number to keep it from rusting and spotting. Metal can also be wiped down with rubbing

alcohol and wiped with a damp cloth. And keep metal away from your glass toys to avoid breakage—they go together like opera and Britney Spears. In fact, keep them away from all other toys, with the batteries out, because even nonrusting metals can rust *each other* if they come in contact, or the batteries inside them can rust. See also **storage**.

Mile-High Kit, the

Luggage can make or break travel, and this kit's sleek carrying case, in tangerine or silver, is cool and convenient. Throw it in your weekend suitcase and go! Comes with scented cloths, a tin of hot cinnamon mints, a folding pocket mirror, a **blindfold**, bottles of **massage oil** and personal **lubricant**, a feather tickler (which may sound cheesy but actually feels rilly good), a mini personal massager (i.e., a **miniature vibrator**), three condoms, a "pleasure ring" (so ➔

much nicer sounding than "cock **ring**"), and the requisite "Do not disturb" door hanger (available all over; $$). Also comes in a mini version with half the stuff at half the size and half the price. Either makes a great gift. (And they didn't even pay us to say that!) See also **beginner toys** and **kits**.

miniature vibrators

A miniature vibrator, sometimes known as a **bullet vibrator**, is exactly what it sounds like: a teeny-tiny buzzing toy. Typically 1 to 2 inches long and less than 1 inch across, these vibes *can* be used on their own, but they're much more commonly employed to add vibrations to something else: a **butt plug**, a **cock ring**, a **dildo**, a **harness**, **nipple clamps**, etc.

Cordless bullets with watch batteries give you the greatest freedom of mobility, but the batteries themselves can be expensive and tend to run out quickly (though here's a handy hint: Buy the batteries at sex stores, where they tend to be much cheaper than at watch stores). Bullets with regular battery packs usually give you more control options and come with a belt clip that you could hang on a **harness**, but there are some drawbacks: The cord can easily get tangled between two moving bodies, there's always a temptation to tug on the cord (which risks damaging the vibe), and regular batteries, though cheaper than watch batteries, can wear out the vibe motor faster (so go with no-name brands over stronger Energizers to help the vibe last longer). We like the One-Touch (or Magic Touch) Mini Bullet, GV's wireless Itty Bitty vibe (a.k.a. BL's wireless Zippy), and—the tiniest out there at 1 inch by ½ inch— **Vibratex**'s battery-pack Red Zinger (BF, MP; BL calls it Red Hots). That said, you can find a wide selection of miniature vibes in *any* of the sex-toy shops discussed in this book, and quality and price ($) tend to be pretty consistent across the board.

If you're going to use a miniature vibe unadorned—maybe you like its very focused approach—it's best used externally: The wireless bullets could easily get lost up there—*obviously*—and the wired ones aren't strong enough to tug on. If you do want to use it in the vagina, slip it inside a condom so you can pull on the condom, rather than the wire, when you're done playing. Even then, keep it out of your butt, please, lest you end up with a bullet vibe *and* a condom stranded somewhere up near your colon. To dress your bullet up in something besides a condom, see **miniature-vibrator sleeves** following. See also **boy toys**, **butterfly vibrators with harnesses**, **Feeldoe double dildos**, and **Tristan 2**.

miniature-vibrator sleeves

These are like cozies for a **miniature vibrator**, and there are more of them for sale than we care to mention. As with the mini vibes, they're sold everywhere, and price and quality are fairly consistent. Some are **jelly**, some are **Cyberskin** or fleshlike material, some have fronds, some have bumps, some have bunny ears, some are dolphins, some are tongue shaped, some cup over a penis (see the SWAK sleeve in the **boy toys** entry)—and most cost less than ten bucks. The basic idea is to help diffuse the vibrations in a more "interesting" fashion. As with the mini vibes, they should never go in the bum, and they should be inserted into the vagina only if they're inside a condom. Actually, seeing as most of them are made of jelly, a condom's always a good idea anyway. Or just buy them from A-Womans-Touch where they're all **silicone**, **vinyl**, or **latex**. Can't make up your mind? Get an Itty Bitty Kit with a vibe

→

and *five* jelly sleeves (GV; $$)! It's okay—sex-toy shopping makes gluttons out of the best of us. FYI, you can also get textured **sleeves** for your **Pocket Rocket** or Water Dancer vibrators.

Mistress dildo

See **dildos**.

monogamous toy

A sex toy used by only one person, never shared with another, to avoid the spread of STDs and bad bacteria. However, if you have a committed, monogamous partner with whom you are body-fluid bonded, then sharing a toy just between the two of you is okey-dokey.

MyPleasure .com

Another friendly online retailer featuring the usual: a wide selection of toys, shopping guides, customer reviews, staff product picks, sex and romance tips, and expert advice from two licensed sex therapists (Dr. Sandor Gardos and Dr. Linda R. Mona—or should that be Moan-ah?). But what sets them apart is what you *won't* find: explicit DVDs, live demonstration workshops, nudity or offensive imagery, or any particular political views (that means no don't-trust-the-Man warnings about **phthalates** in **jelly** toys). Unfortunately, you won't find inviting design, helpful navigation, or very thorough health info, either. But their prices are industry standard, and they don't accept outside advertising. They say the very first e-mail they ever received was from a lonely, eighty-something widow who had ordered her first-ever toy from them because MP was the only store that didn't appall her; turns out she'd never had an orgasm before and was writing to thank them for giving her that experience before she died. Check out their one and only exclusive toy, the **Pure Bliss vibrator**.

N

nail file

You might not think this belongs in your sex-toy chest, but that's because you've never felt a hang-nail you-know-where. This is a public service announcement: If you're going in the vagina or up the ass, please file your nails first! And no precariously attached Lee Press-Ons, either. A nail file is also good for smoothing out the seams or manufacturing flaws of your cheap **plastic** or **acrylic** toys.

naming toys

People name their cars, their boats, their houses, their laptops, their genitalia—why not their sex toys? Certainly, the names they come with lack subtlety—who'd want to invite the Super Duper Ballsy Dong into their bedroom? Puh-lease. Sex toys can be nicknamed with more abandon than one's own family jewels (because you're not stuck with them for life). Some toys are crying out for an ironic, porn-inspired moniker like the Pounder or Debbie. Single women in particular are wont to give their favorite toy a pet name, like Chad, as in, "What are you doing on Saturday?" "Oh, you know, I'll probably just order in and watch a movie with Chad." In such cases, it is seemly to retire this nickname when one wishes to introduce Chad to a new, flesh-and-blood partner.

Natural Contours toys

This line of **contour toys**, designed in conjunction with porn-for-chicks producer Candida Royalle, would look more at home on your cosmetics shelf than in your **vibrator** collection. There are no sharp edges or corners on these toys—they're designed to fit comfortably around or inside a woman's body, and the external vibrators can even fit comfortably between partners during sex, thanks to ➔

their ergonomic curves. Entirely unthreatening, they're great for nervous nellies who aren't sure whether they're the sex-toy type: discreet, quiet, gentle, and completely unrealistic (i.e., not a single one bears the remotest resemblance to a penis!). Magnifique is their largest and most popular vibrator, and can be used either internally or externally. Ultime penetrates for **G-spot** access while also stimulating the **clitoris**; Liberté is just for G-spotting. Energie is their widely revered **kegel** exerciser—it's made of **metal**, for the weight, then covered in plastic to avoid that cold speculum feeling. It's enough to make you forgive them the dorky French-wannabe names, oui? These **nonporous** plastic toys are all battery operated (AA) and can be wiped clean with a damp, soapy cloth. They're available everywhere, or you can order directly from Natural-Contours.com. All are in the $$ range, cheapest at BF! Hey, we're on nobody's side but yours. See also **contour toys**, **Emotional Bliss**, and **Pure Bliss vibrator**.

Nexus double dildos

The Nexus, by **Vixen Creations**, comes in two models: the original Nexus and (by popular demand) Nexus Junior. The driver's end of both Nexus models is longer and wider than on the **Feeldoe double dildo** and has a realistic head—some lady drivers find the Nexus easier to grip onto because of this, while others prefer the stubbier, more bulbous-headed Feeldoe. Both double dongs provide **G-spot** stimulation and ridges for **clitoris** attention, and the poking ends are very similar on both the Feeldoe and the Nexus. The main difference between the two is the angle: The Nexus is built on a 90-degree angle, as opposed to the Feeldoe's 45-degree angle. This angle means that the Nexus is harder to keep in place, and you may find that you need to employ the help of a **harness** or a pair of button-fly jeans. (In general, women seem to find that the Feeldoe handles better without

a harness than the Nexus does.) But if you have super-fly PC muscles (see **kegels**), you may well prove us wrong on that front. This toy is pure **silicone**: boil or wash. Don't forget the water-based **lube**! It's available everywhere for $$$ (WT calls the original one Thelma & Louise and the Junior one Betty & Veronica). See also **dildos** and **dildos, double**.

Night Rider harness

This washable nylon **harness** attaches to anything—and we mean *anything*. Attach it to your favorite inanimate object—coffee table, desk, door, (stationary) motorbike, washing machine— insert your favorite silicone **dildo**, and hump away. We must insist, however, that you not strap it to a pet. (BL; $$.) See also **harnesses, thigh** and **strap-ons**.

nipple clamps, about

Why would you want a tool to pinch your nips? Because pain feels a lot like pleasure when you're really turned on. And because reducing the circulation in your nips increases sensitivity—like, a *lot*. The most blasé nipples have been known to blossom into full-on erogenous zones with the aid of a little clamping. And the pain subsides after you've been clamped for a while—it's like icing a sprained ankle: Eventually, your body just stops freaking out about the cold and gets numb to it. Though remember that circulation is your body's life force, so never clamp for more than

➔

ten to fifteen minutes at a time. (And even less time than that if you notice anything getting blue or cold.)

When applying the clamps, think back to playground fights: The less skin you pinch, the more it hurts, and the bigger and wider the clamps are, the less they'll hurt. You can apply to places other than the nips: Some people like to attach them to their labia or their ball sac or, more randomly, their earlobes. You can also go **DIY** with some **clothespins**.

The craziest feeling comes when you release the nipple clamps. The sudden rush of blood back to the area hurts like a mother, which, as we said, can be a good thing—in context. (And when is sex *not* about context? Take your O-face, for example. How tardo does *that* look out of context?) If the sudden pain is too much, you can slow down the return of blood by pressing your palm or fingers to the nipples in question. After this release, the nips will remain extra sensitive for a while. If that's a bad thing, just ice them down. If that's a

good thing—well, we think you know what to do. See also **pumps, clitoral & nipple**.

nipple clamps, clover

These Japanese-style clamps (\$ on BF) are known as such due to their popularity in **Japanese** bondage films. Clover clamps get tighter as you pull on the chain, which makes them perfect for a little power play: The more you resist, the more it hurts. (What's that they say about resistance being futile?)

nipple clamps, tweezer

For a slightly softer touch than the clover clamps, go with the tweezer kind, which look like a set of tweezers on a string. They've got rubber tips and are *completely* adjustable, so you can start with a very light squeeze. You can test the grip on your inner wrist. Grab the nipple close to the base, or even on the areola, for a gentler hold. Tweezer clamps are attached by a chain, which you can use to lightly tug on the clamps, add weights, or yank off the clamps in one fell swoop. Some versions, called "Y chains," have a third chain and clamp, which extends down to the clitoris. (Available at most sex-toy shops; $.)

clamps (available at most sex-toy stores; $$). These have a looser grip, so they won't *completely* cut off circulation, while the vibration will raise your sensitivity level enough to make your nipples the star of the show.

nipple jewelry

The best way to adorn your rosebuds without hardcore piercing or clamping. There are rings that simply hang off erect nipples, or jewelry that encircles the nipple (one brand is called Nipple-Huggers.com; $), or stainless-steel nipple shields à la Janet Jackson (EB; $$), or mini nipple cuffs that screw around the tip of the nip (a pair with brass hoops at WT sells for $$).

nipple clamps, vibrating & pulsating

If numb nips aren't your cup of tea, you might want to think about vibrating or pulsating

nipple pumps

See **pumps, clitoral & nipple**.

nipple suction cups

Also called nipple suckers or sucklers, these are small, often clear, tubular suction cups that bring blood to the surface quickly, increasing sensitivity like a **nipple clamp** does. However, the pace is less violent than when removing clamps. But remember, the fifteen-minute rule applies to these, too. WT's Nipple Sucklers with connective chain sell for $$. By the way, if you happen to have a snakebite kit handy, you can use its venom-extracting suction cups for the same saucy result.

Nonoxynol-9

Nonoxynol-9 is a spermicide found in some contraceptive jellies, **condoms**, and **lubes**. Years ago, lab tests found that Nonoxynol-9 kills HIV—in the *lab*—so manufacturers started adding it willy-nilly to lubes and condoms. Unfortunately, N-9 is not quite so helpful *outside* the

lab; in fact, it can actually cause tiny tears in the lining of the vagina and the anus, which would *increase* the risk of transmitting HIV. D'oh! Plus, the amount of N-9 found in lubes and condoms isn't enough to prevent pregnancy, and many women find the ingredient incredibly irritating down there. That was enough for us: None of the lubes or condoms recommended in this book contains N-9. Some sex-toy outlets—BL and GV, for example—don't even stock any lubes or condoms that contain N-9. But many retailers don't think it's a big deal; if you do, then be sure to always check the ingredients before you buy.

nonporous

Having a solid surface that will not harbor bacteria or emit chemicals (i.e., the opposite of **porous**). It's definitely a quality you want to look for in a sex toy. **Materials** that are nonporous include *hard* **acrylic**, *hard* **elastomer**, **glass**, **metals**, and **silicone**.

novelties

You might think this word means "nice, fun sex toys," but you'd be wrong. It's actually a legal term for products not intended for serious use. And thanks to bull-shitty obscenity laws still on the books in some states (every-thing's dumber in Texas), no government regulation of sex toys, and manufacturers who focus on quantity over quality, most toys in your average adult store are marked "for novelty purposes only" (read: "Don't use this anywhere near your genitals!"). As novelties, they don't come with instruction manuals or ingredients listings; if they did, they'd be considered medical devices and would be subject to expensive safety reg-ulations. "Fuck that," say the big-biz manufacturers. "We'll just keep doing what we've been doing for the past thirty years, thank you very much." (Good for them, bad for you.)

These novelty items are actually the old-timers of the sex-toy world. Back in the sixties and the early seventies, before there existed female-friendly shops like **Eve's Garden**, **Good Vibrations**, and **Babeland**, the driving force in product development was gimmick. Sure, vibrators had been around since the Victorian era, thanks to a serious misdiagnosis of **hysteria**, but almost a century later, sexism continued to hamper sex toys' ability to get the job done (talk about one hundred years of solitude). Both sex shops and the products they stocked were designed with men in mind (and we're not even going to start on the people who worked there), which meant that vibrators were cheap, plastic affairs with no more intent to please a woman than a frat boy after six shots of Jager. (And, in fact, most novelty toys have about the same staying power as a soused frat boy, too.)

As we mentioned above, you can still find these products today, not only in the kind of sex-toy shop that makes you feel a bit dirty—and not the good kind of dirty—but also in more female-friendly stores, because they are *soooo* inexpensive (and

➜

many people just aren't used to the idea of investing in their own sex lives yet). You'll often find the novelty toys sharing shelf space with other low-brow items such as Anal-Eze **desensitizer**, "pussy tighteners," and a cream called Sta-hard [*sic*]. Novelty toys are basically the Victoria's Secret of the sex-toy world—i.e., they work with a definition of *sexy* that exists mostly in boys' wet dreams. As for a woman's own definition of sexy? Fuggedaboudit. For one step backward, see **gag gifts**. For toys that are truly novel without being trashy, see **undercover toys**.

Nubby G vibrator

Don't believe in the **G-spot**? Well, Virginia, this battery-operated toy—alias Jelly-G—may well convert you. This **jelly rubber** innie **vibrator** features a significant curve to reach the G-spot (hers *or* his) and a nubby ring at the base that stimulates the **clit**/anus/**perineum** as you rock the toy back and forth. The vibrations can feel pretty intense in there, even on the lowest setting, so it's not for everyone— it depends what kind of action your G gets off on (if, indeed, it gets off on anything at all). The basic model is 4½ inches by 1⅜ inches; it also comes in a junior version and a waterproof version. Made of **jelly**, so clean with mild soap and water and use with a condom, whether it's monogamous or you're sharing, because of **phthalates**. (If you're in the mood for condom-free G-hunting, check out the **Pixie vibrator** instead.) The Nubby G is available at BL and MP (as the Nubby G), GV (as the Crystal Jelly Deluxe), or LB (as the Classic G) for $.

P

P-spot

The male G-spot. It's a just-because present for guys who have an open backdoor policy. It's more clinically known as the **prostate**, which is why some people refer to it as the P-spot, and is located about 3 inches in from his anus. To find your partner's magic button, have him lie on his back and insert your well-**lubed** index finger, palm up, almost all the way in, aiming for the navel. (Be sure to file your nail first! Or use **latex gloves**.) Then curve your finger in a come-hither gesture and rub his walnut-size nubbin of lovin' ever so gently. If your male partner has the backdoor jitters (hey, we've all been there), you may need to work up to his G-spot: Start with a brief **perineum** massage during one sesh, then next time rub just the surface of his starfish, and maybe the time after that go in just half an

inch, and so on. Chances are, these anal attempts will be best received if you happen to be giving him a blow job at the time. A little Pavlovian conditioning never hurt anyone. See also **anal play**, and **G-spot stimulators (his & hers)**.

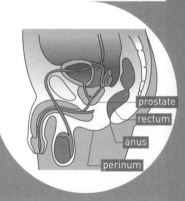

packing

See **softpacks**.

paddles

If you've always wanted to try a good old-fashioned schoolteacher spanking but are embarrassed about your limp →

wrist, or if you can't think of a nice way to tell your partner that he or she spanks like a wet noodle, a paddle is your friend in need. Paddles have a comfortingly low kink factor (that is, if you find a lot of **leather** and latex *un*comfortable). Put it this way: If the Gap sold **whips**, babyGap would stock paddles. In fact, many happy paddlers never venture any further into the world of **BDSM**—it's not necessarily a gateway toy, no matter what the anti-kink brigade would have you think. A spanking paddle can be made of wood, leather, **vinyl**, or rubber, and it looks kind of like a Ping-Pong paddle (though it may be larger). In fact, now that we think of it, a Ping-Pong paddle would make a *fine* spanking apparatus.

Different kinds of paddles provide varying spanking experiences: A thick, heavy paddle will impart a satisfying thud, while a thinner, lighter paddle (sometimes called a slapper) will give more of a smack. The more rodlike the paddle, the more of a sting it will yield.

For the bipolar spanker, try a paddle that's leather on one side and fleece on the other (BF; $$). If you fancy yourself a bit of an artist, you might enjoy one of the paddles with heart or star shapes on them (GV, BL, MP; about $$$)—if you wield it just so, you'll leave a nice imprint on your spankee's ass. It's like toast stenciling for grown-ups!

Speaking of kitchen appliances: Your kitchen is chock-full of potential **DIY** paddles: A wooden spoon, a small chopping board, a wooden scrubbing brush, a spatula—washing up was never so much fun. We've also heard that hard-soled slippers make handy-dandy paddles, just in case your ultimate fantasy involves a crotchety old grandpa who's pissed that you broke his window playing ball.

Ready for your just desserts? Try bending over your partner's lap—that position could be all the role-playing you need. (Or—you never know—the position might inspire you to new role-playing heights. Scene!) If you're the spanker, never paddle someone anywhere near bones:

→

Aim for the fleshy part of their bum only (if they don't have a fleshy part on the bum, make them a sandwich instead). The ass cheeks are safe *and* sexy—a good thud back there will send tingles throughout the genitals. Build up gradually—you can even start off by paddling your partner over jeans or underwear while you get used to your spanker of choice. See also **canes**, **floggers**, **riding crop**, and **whips**.

boots in *Pretty Woman*). Or perhaps your shiny patent leather **paddle** holds a special place in your heart because it reminds you of those patent leather Mary Jane party shoes your third-grade crush was wearing when she beat you up in the school courtyard. For **vegetarians** who want to get in on the action, there is poromeric imitation **leather**, with a similarly glossy appearance. Both are cleaned by wiping down with a damp cloth, adding a mild soap if need be. You can buy purpose-made patent leather and poromeric cleaners to help remove minor scuffs.

PC muscle

See **pelvic floor muscles**.

patent leather

Material frequently used for sex accessories and fetish clothing, due to its hooker-lite aesthetic (see Julia Roberts'

pelvic floor muscles

A group of muscles (which includes the pubococcygeus, or PC muscle, and the bulbo-cavernosus muscle) that helps

→

P

hold the pelvic organs in place and provides support for other internal organs all the way up to your diaphragm, in both men and women. They relax and contract during arousal and orgasm, peeing and pooing, and, in women, childbirth. A woman's pelvic muscles pass around the urethra, the clitoris, the vagina, and the anus, so you can see how sensations can cross and overlap down there. For women, strong pelvic floor muscles can mean stronger orgasms or even orgasms, period (not to mention less chance of incontinence later in life). Men might notice improved O's, too, though the effect is less dramatic. You can strengthen them by doing **kegel** exercises (see that entry for specific strengthening toys). For some good diagrams and further descriptions of these muscles, check out Rebecca Chalker's book *The Clitoral Truth*.

penis

The male analog of the **clitoris**. There aren't nearly as many toys for the penis as there are for the clit (probably because it's really hard to compete with one's own hand and a little bit of lube), but the options are improving: cock **rings**, **masturbation sleeves** (including the popular **Fleshlight**), **porn-star toys**, a **RealDoll**—okay, maybe *improving* is a poor choice of word. See also **boy toys**.

penis enlargement

A penis-size serenity prayer: "Grant me the serenity to accept the things I cannot change, the courage to change the things I can, and the wisdom to know the difference." Need some exegesis? What you cannot change: Your penis size. Seriously, dudes: Stop opening all that penis spam! We know the e-mail subject lines threaten your very manhood, but it wouldn't be an epidemic if so many of you didn't keep clicking on links like "larger ur damn small di-ck with plaster," "No More lonliness, add

3+ inches," "NEW: The penis pill is proven to add inches," "SuperSize Your Schlong," and our personal fave, "The mighty cucumber lives again!"

Let's say it together, shall we? There is no safe way to enlarge your number-one guy. Pills, creams, weights, exercises, jelquing, stretching racks that resemble medieval torture devices—it's all one big scam. Surgery *might* help increase your *flaccid* length and width—big whoop. Flaccid improvements don't do shit in the sack. And are you really that concerned about your rep in the communal shower at the gym? (Don't answer that, gay guys.) Here's something you should be concerned about: The high rate of botched jobs in the field of penile-enlargement surgery.

Next time you're having a bad penis day, check out Web sites like ErectionPhotos.com and Measurection.com to see how you *really* measure up.

What you can change: your penis size—temporarily. See penis **extenders** and penis **pumps**.

How to know the difference: If something is recommended in this book, gather your courage and give it a shot. If it's not, accept with serenity that a gross penile malformation is a big price to pay for an extra quarter-inch.

penis pumps

See **pumps, penis**.

perineum

T'aint the ass and t'aint the balls—it's the perineum! Otherwise known as, you guessed it, the "taint." This is the short stretch of skin starting below the balls in men and below the vulva in women and extending, in both cases, back to the anus. Men in particular often enjoy gentle pressure on this spot, which can indirectly stimulate their **P-spot** (a.k.a. **prostate**). A.k.a. the runway, the chin rest.

phthalates

A class of chemicals mainly used as "plasticizers"—i.e., substances added to plastics (like PVC, see **vinyl**) to increase their flexibility and softness (to make, for example, **jelly rubber**). Phthalates—pronounced "THALL-eights" or "THAY-lates," depending on who you ask— are found in a huge variety of consumer products such as decorating and building products, cosmetics, hairspray, deodorant, wood finishes, insecticides, and—surprise, surprise—sex toys! Products with phthalates reek—kind of like that new-car smell—because their chemistry is unstable and they are "outgassing" (releasing vapors).

Most studies to date have been performed on animals and show that large amounts of phthalates can damage their organs. The latest studies indicate that phthalates can interfere with hormones and may reduce sperm count, cause testicular cancer, or counteract breast cancer medicines. Baby- and pet-product manufacturers in the United States have voluntarily eliminated phthalates from their products (in Canada and Europe, they're banned outright from those products). "Adult" toys, on the other hand? They're not regulated by the government. And manufacturers criticize these studies, claiming that the methodology used (using unrealistically high dosages on animals that are way more sensitive than humans, or, in human testing, using small, homogenous study groups that are not pulled from a wide variety of regions) cannot definitively claim widespread problems related to phthalates.

But check this out: A few years ago, the Canadian Broadcasting Corporation (the Canuck national public broadcaster) reported findings from German chemist Hans Ulrich Krieg, who had been analyzing the contents of consumer goods, including sex toys, for years. Krieg found that ten dangerous chemicals gassed out of toys, the most dangerous being phthalates. They were found in concentrations of up

P

→

to 243,000 parts per million (ppm); in Canada, the tolerable maximum daily exposure is 1,000–3,000 ppm.

Today, many vendors of jelly-rubber sex toys advise covering them in condoms when used internally due to the possible health risks. And at least one, **A-Womans-Touch.com**, refuses to even carry jelly toys, because jelly contains the worst kind of phthalates at the highest levels. In fact, WT works with a chemist who tests every kind of toy they sell for phthalates. Most of the toys WT sells are completely phthalate free; the rest contain phthalates only at extremely low levels and contain none of the top ten worst kinds of phthalates, so the chemist considers them safe for use. Therefore, if you're ever confused about a toy, here's a good rule of thumb: If you can find it at WT, you know it's been through a pretty rigorous testing process. And until the government decides to step in and regulate this freakin' industry, that's the best you can hope for. We know, science is hard.

Pixie vibrator

The first vibe to mimic the come-hither movement favored by **G-spot** enthusiasts (see **Pro-Touch**). This pink **Vibratex** toy also vibrates and is covered with hundreds of soft and squishy nubbins. Its hook shape may be a little intimidating at first, but once you get it in your V, you'll be impressed by the finger-stroking simulation. Even if you hate having your G-spot prodded, you still might enjoy it by flipping it over so it stimulates your rectum *indirectly* (never insert anally). It's not that quiet, and if you're prone to really clenching your vaginal and **PC muscles**, the piston action can actually be incapacitated. →

P

It's made of Vibratex's own high-quality brand of **elastomer**, so that means it's **latex** and **phthalate** free, but that also means it's **porous**. If you're going to share it, always slap a **condom** on it, but if you make it a **monogamous toy**, **clean** it very carefully, and **store** it properly, you should be able to enjoy all those nubbins condom free without consequence. Available for extra dough with a clitoral attachment on a cord ($$ at BF; $$$ at DS and BL).

plastic, hard

Hard, cold, completely inflexible—plastic is the material exes are made of. Plastic's not great for the environment, but so few sex-toy **materials** are. Vibe motors encased in hard plastic really give off strong vibrations, since there's no soft material to absorb the shock. Plastic toys are usually fine for external stim, but often not so great for internal use or thrusting because, even though hard plastic is **nonporous** and **phthalate**-free, it can have

jagged and bacteria-friendly seams, it may have a metallic coating (which could flake off), and many plastic toys feature cords (like in the case of some **bullet vibrators**) that should not be tugged on. If you're going to insert it somewhere, use a **condom**! (A better version of hard plastic is hard **acrylic**.) Plastic can be wiped down with rubbing alcohol followed by a water rinse or just washed with soap and water.

plastic, soft

Soft **elastomer**, **jelly rubber**, and **vinyl**—all **materials** that are **porous**.

Pocket Rocket vibrator

Of the smaller-size vibes, this is the Biggie. It's sold practically everywhere. Made by **Doc Johnson**, the Pocket Rocket is large enough to hold in your hand and pack a decent vibratory punch (unlike some **miniature** →

vibrators) and small enough to just throw in your purse and go (unlike, say, the **Thunder Cloud dual-action vibrator**). Having a bad day at the office? Just sneak off to the bathroom, press it against your happy place (external only), and feel the stress just melt away. Some versions even come with three interchangeable tops for different clit stim, or you can buy one of many **miniature-vibrator sleeves** to dress it up.

Though the Pocket Rocket has a catchy, kick-ass moniker, **Vibratex**'s waterproof version is a better bet, despite its cornball name: the Water Dancer vibrator. Made by this smaller, more quality-conscious company, the Water Dancer is easier to clean, and you can take it in the shower (just be careful to keep the battery compartment closed and dry). If you add the **jelly** rabbit **sleeve** for another $10 or so (which also fits the Pocket Rocket, natch), it's called the Rabbit Dancer. Both are quiet and require only one—count it, *one*—AA battery. The Pocket Rocket Jr. is half the length,

comes with a handy wrist cord, and is waterproof. (It's not called the Water Dancer Jr. because it's made by Doc Johnson.) Vibratex's Titan is the slightly longer, slightly stronger (two batteries), and therefore slightly pricier version of the Water Dancer. (Doc Johnson's taller version is called the Pocket Missile.) None of the toys in this range should be inserted anywhere: They are all for external use only. The PR and WD are available everywhere ($).

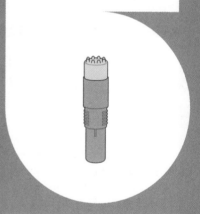

porn-star toys

Toys for porno "swimfans" and John Hinckley Jrs. There are lines of toys branded after certain →

P

porn stars and toys made from actual molds of certain porn stars' various disembodied anatomical parts (mouths, vaginas, penises, anuses). For example, Jenna Jameson has lent her name, image, and form to **Doc Johnson** for a vibrating mouth, a vibrating vagina-ass combo (for missionary-position view), a vibrating ass-vagina combo (for doggy-style view, 'cause you gotta have *both*), a masturbation sleeve that we're sure looks nothing like her veegee, and even a vibrating virtual doll with a *removable* vagina and ass (only $200!), available on Edenfantasys.com. In **Japan**, you can buy inflatable "love pillows" featuring life-size pictures of porn stars or anime characters and an optional hole for wholly unlifelike poking. See also **RealDoll**.

porous

Having a surface with pores that will harbor bacteria and may emit chemicals (i.e., the opposite of **nonporous**). It's a quality you should try to avoid in a sex toy whenever possible—when you don't avoid it, you'll need to clean the toy carefully and either keep it **monogamous** or use it with a **condom**. (And if it's one of the many porous toys that contains **phthalates**, you'll need to use a condom either way.) **Materials** that are porous include soft **elastomer**, **jelly rubber**, **latex rubber**, and **vinyl**.

P

Pro-Touch vibrating butt plug

Among butt toys, this **Tantus** product is one of the popular kids. Have you ever heard someone say that the way to a woman's vaginal **G-spot** or a man's rectal **P-spot** is to make a come-hither motion with your finger inside those canals, aimed toward the navel? Well, this butt plug looks like an extra-large finger (5 inches by 1¼ inches) making that gesture (so it can do double duty as a G-spot toy for her). For more operating instructions, see **anal play** and **butt plugs**. Pro-Touch is made of 100 percent **silicone**, so wash or boil to clean (remove the vibe first!), and use with a water-based lube. Available at BL, BF, DS, and GV ($).

prostate

A gland of the male sex organs that secretes fluid that is part of the semen concoction. Known as the **P-spot** when referred to in a sexual context. See the P-spot entry for more details on its location and stimulation.

pumps, clitoral & nipple

Pumps aren't just for penises: Try one out on your nipples or the number-one clit in your life, too. The effect isn't quite as dramatic as it would be on a penis, of course, but the device will nevertheless draw blood to the area being pumped, which mimics the arousal process and makes everything even more sensitive to touch. Many women love the feeling of suction on the **clitoris** (especially those women who kinda like having their blood pressure taken—you know who you are), and some women with sexual dysfunction actually *need* it. (The FDA approved a device for female sexual dysfunction →

called the Eros CTD that doctors can prescribe.) Plus, once you've pumped, you've got a (temporarily) extra-large clitoris to play with, too! The cheapest nipple and clit pumps are plastic ($$).

The **Berman Center** came out with its own based on the Eros called the Selene (**EvesGarden .com**; $$). Or, if you want to get a bit fancy, BL and GV both sell **Lucite** one-handed pumps ($$) that can be attached to a nipple and clit cylinder (sold separately; $$). If you want to go in on the purchase with your boyfriend, this fancy pump can also be attached to a penis cylinder (BL, GV; $$$). See also **nipple clamps**; **nipple suction cups**; and **pumps, penis**.

pumps, penis

You know how really organized people pack just the right amount of stuff for their luggage, while the rest of us have to jump up and down on our suitcase to get it to close? That's kind of like the penis pump. With an ordinary erection (not

that *any* erection is ordinary—don't get us wrong, fellas), blood flows into the penis, causing it to stand to attention. A pump, on the other hand, *forces* the blood in, creating an erection on demand—it's what docs used to prescribe before the magic blue pill came along.

A pumped-up stiffie (a.k.a. an Ah-nold) will be all that you can be, because it pushes the maximum amount of blood in there—so if you are prone to less-than-fully-inflated erections, a pump will probably make you feel bigger. Of course, this lasts only for as long as the erection itself—once your schlong has deflated, you'll be left with the same old penis, except it might be a little tender and maybe even bruised. Or, if you pump for too long or too often or too vigorously, the pump might cause burst capillaries, tissue damage, ligament damage at the penis base, or lymph blisters on the head of the penis. (Hey, don't shoot the fine-print messenger.) Some gentlemen also report that they find it, er, *harder* to ejaculate with an Ah-nold.

P

These devices work by creating a vacuum around your trouser snake—**lubing** up first will help seal this vacuum. Besides, anytime you're sliding something over your dong, it's a good idea to lubricate. Also, don't pump for more than ten minutes without taking a break—that's more abuse than any penis should be forced to take.

The penis pumps you'll find in sex-toy shops aren't medical grade, and they shouldn't be considered a fall-back plan if you're too embarrassed to talk to your doctor about erectile dysfunction. (Come on, if Bob Dole can do it . . .) The novelty pumps, like the **Fireman's Pump**, are meant only as a masturbation prop or as a pre-sex stupid human trick (adding a cock **ring** to your Ah-nold may help maintain it longer). Speaking of your doctor, don't use a pump, even for novelty purposes—ready for more fine print?—if you bleed easily, have a blood-clotting disorder, are diabetic, suffer from any peripheral vascular disease, or take anti-coagulants, aspirin, or any other blood-thinning medication. If something feels funny down there, suck it up and tell your doc what you did. See also **pumps, clitoral & nipple**.

Pure Bliss vibrator

MP has a great little toy—their only exclusive one—that's an **undercover** vibe disguised as a mini neck and **"back" massager** but designed for the nether regions. It's no **high-end sex toy** ($$), but it comes in a nice box, is whisper quiet, and has strong vibrations, making it a good deal for a **contour toy**.

PVC

See **vinyl**.

Pyrex

A brand name for high-quality **glass**.

Q

queening stools

Low seats that open the sitter to oral attention from the person lying below, often employed in **BDSM** play. A.k.a. smotherboxes. See also **erotic furniture**.

R

Rabbit Habit & Rabbit Pearl vibrators

Probably the most widely recognized vibe in the world, thanks in large part to the *Sex and the City* episode in which prudish Charlotte gets so **addicted** to her battery-powered, floppy-eared companion that her friends stage a vibrator intervention. The Rabbit Habit and the Rabbit Pearl (available most everywhere; $$-$$$ depending on retailer) are both **dual-action** vibrators by **Vibratex** that boast a swirling shaft, undulating pearls inside the base for stimulation of the sensitive **vaginal** opening, and an external rabbit whose ears flutter against the clitoris. There's so much going on, this vibe does everything *but* your dishes! You can vary both the vibration intensity and swirling speed with the controls at either the base of

→

the unit (Habit; illustrated) or on the battery pack attached by a cord (Pearl).

The Rabbit is a **Japanese**-made, high-performance product—it's not going to crap out on you, unlike its cheap knock-offs (such as **California Exotic Novelties**' Jack Rabbit, among others). The only bummer: It's made of **vinyl**. Though the Vibratex kind is much higher quality (i.e., less porous) than most and deemed safe by **A-Womans-Touch.com**'s chemist, it's still made with **phthalates** and can harbor bacteria, so you might want to use a **condom** with it—definitely, if you're sharing. For this reason, we're going to commit sex-toy blasphemy and say there are several very similar dual-action vibes that are *better than the Rabbit*:

Twist & Shake series: These three cordless vibes from **Fun Factory** all have a rotating shaft, undulating beads, and an external clit stimulator, but they are made of premium **silicone**—which makes these babies the best of the bunch. There's the inchworm-shaped Paul & Pauline, the Mary Mermaid, with tail-fin clit stim, and the Sally Sea, shaped like two seals—all in a variety of bright solid colors. Their shafts are 5 inches by 1½ inches, and they use four AA batteries apiece ($$$).

Original Deluxe Japanese Butterfly: One of several new cordless thermoplastic **elastomer** dual-action vibes from **Vibratex**—the toy is lighter than a silicone equivalent, **latex** free (for those with allergies), and phthalate free (yay, no seeping toxins!) but **porous**. It's got everything the Rabbit has, plus more girth (the shaft is 4 inches by 1⅝ inches), an accordion-shaped head, and a freaking light inside! Understandably, it's one of Vibratex's biggest sellers. (It's called the Flutter Vibe on WT and the Rock Lobster on BL; $$$.)

Quiver: Another of Vibratex's variable-speed elastomer toys. It's got a clit attachment that's more substantial than most (which may give you more diffused clit stim), a shaft with a bigger, bulbous head, and, instead of beads, tiny tentacles sprouting from the iridescent

→

R

material. Its shaft is 4 inches by 1½ inches, and it takes four AA batteries (BF; $$$).

Rock Your World: This Vibratex elastomer toy, like the Quiver, looks funky, with similar (though fewer) soft spikes protruding from its surface. The shaft is ribbed and slightly **bendable** to the angle of your liking. Same size as the Quiver, but requires only three AA batteries. (BL sells it as the Space Invader; $$$.)

And, drum roll, please . . .

The Phthalate-Free Rabbit: Vibratex has made a new version of their signature vibe with their new **elastomer**. Yippee! (Now, let's just keep our fingers crossed for a silicone one down the road—which they've told us they're looking into.)

See also **Thunder Cloud dual-action vibrator**.

RealDoll

Realdoll.com's spiel: "Since 1996, we have been using Hollywood special effects technology to produce the most realistic love doll in the world. Our dolls feature completely articulated skeletons, which allow for anatomically correct positioning, an exclusive blend of the most expensive silicone rubbers for an ultra fleshlike feel, and are each custom made to order, to our customer's specifications. We offer an extensive list of options, from body type and face type all the way down to fingernail color. If you've ever dreamed of creating your ideal woman, then you have come to the right place." Still not clear? They're pimped-up mannequins you can fuck, tell your fears to, punch in the face, take to a drive-in movie—if this wasn't a judgment-free zone, we'd say they're toad-licking crazy.

R

receiver's choice

When choosing a strap-on **harness** and **dildo**, the giver may pick the harness he or she finds most comfortable and/or aesthetically pleasing (purple crushed velvet may or may not qualify as either), but the receiver *always* chooses the dildo. Givers, we don't care how long you've been pining for a 7 inch-long, 3-inch-wide purple glittery schlong: Do not stamp your feet like Veruca Salt and demand it *now*. And no passive-aggressive "challenge" moves either, like, "Well, *you're* bigger than that, and I take you back there at least once a week." Shut up and count your blessings that you're not dating some tight-assed corporate lawyer with a roadblock sign at his **perineum**.

rechargeable toys

The wave of the future: no cords to get in the way, no batteries to throw away! Some come with docking stations (**Fun Factory** and **Emotional Bliss** toys), and others come with small jacks, just like a cell phone (like **Lelo vibrators**). Right now, it's mostly just the **high-end sex toys** that offer this, but we have faith that soon enough, this option will be available for the little people, too.

remote control toys

Vibes you or your partner can control with a detached remote control. The quintessential remote control accessory is the vibrating panty or thong, made of cotton, Lycra, PVC, or stretchy lace, with a little pouch over the clitoris for inserting a cordless **miniature vibrator**. The activation range is usually around 12 feet, though some may still work up to 25 feet away. Good if you like a little clitoral stimulation during intercourse and your partner has control issues, or if you two want to spice up a boring holiday office party—zap each other unexpectedly and

→

unbeknownst to your fellow partygoers while they discuss spreadsheets and last night's episode of *Lost*. Variations on this theme include the **Audi-Oh butterfly vibrator**, which is controlled by nearby noise, and the **Vibra-Exciter Cell Phone vibrator**, which is activated by cell phone signals. The panties are available most everywhere, including the **Berman Center** ($$$).

restraints

The tools of bondage: **ball gags**, **bondage belts**, **bondage tape**, **cuffs**, **rope**, **spreader bars**, etc. For a more comprehensive list of all the purpose-made ties that bind, visit **ErosBoutique.com** or **ExtremeRestraints.com**. But if you'd rather go **DIY**, just use a thick necktie, a long sock, a woven leather belt, a winter scarf, or a cotton handkerchief. Contrary to popular belief, silk scarves and stockings aren't all that: They have a tendency to get too tight under tension, making them unsafe and nearly impossible to untie without

cutting off. Avoid thin ropes, twine, thread, and electrical cord, as they're more likely to cut off circulation. Whatever you're using, keep restraints a little loose (especially on joints and pulse points), distribute tension, don't cut off circulation, don't pinch nerve pathways, and make sure the tie-er-upper (if not the one who's tied up) can easily and quickly get the restraints undone in a pinch. Medical scissors with the blunt edges (like the ones you use to cut a kid's toenails) are always good to have on hand. For more info on technique and safety (and you *do* need more if you're new to this), check out *The Erotic Bondage Handbook,* by Jay Wiseman.

riding crops

Long, flexible sticks, usually encased in **leather**, with a handle at one end and a small leather flap on the other used to deliver a stinging slap. Often used by women who had a thing for horses growing up or men too tall to realize their jockeying

R

dreams. Those on the receiving end of a riding crop either enjoy discipline or get off on pretending to be a pony (no joke—they wear saddles on their backs, bits in their mouths, and **butt plugs** with long horsetails attached in their butts). As with any **flogger**, familiarize yourself with the crop's safety guidelines before you go swatting at open flies.

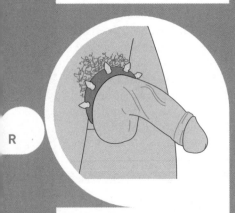

R

rings, cock or penis

There's something about the term "cock ring" that's just so . . . so . . . well, it's got the word *cock* in it, for a start. You may prefer the more pedestrian "penis ring" or "erection ring," or perhaps the slightly whimsical "love ring." Maybe you call your **leather** version a cock ring and your pink, stretchy edition a love ring. Whatever—a rose by any other name, and all that. What's important is what you do with it. Traditionally, a cock ring is meant to strap around a man's penis and behind his balls so that they sit in front of the cock ring, though some men prefer to just place it around the base of the shaft, like a little belt. The idea is to restrict blood flow out of the penis, which *can* lead to harder, longer-lasting, and more sensitive erections. Because blood flows into the penis at its center and flows out through veins closer to the surface, the ring can restrict the outgoing supply without affecting the incoming. Neato! (Note from our lawyers: Cock rings should not be used to treat erectile dysfunction. If you think you may be suffering from erectile dysfunction, talk to your doc.) Of course, penises are as unique as snowflakes

→

(like Grandma always said), so some men will find that the ring *really* affects their sensitivity, causing them to come even sooner, thus overriding the longer-lasting benefit. Others won't notice much difference at all—but, still, it's always nice to accessorize.

rings, materials for

Contrary to popular belief, a cock **ring** does not have to resemble a medieval torture device (though if that's your bag, go for it—just make sure there's a safety release). Cock rings now come in stretchy **Cyberskin** and **jelly rubber** as well as **leather**, **metal**, nylon, rubber, and **silicone**. Some feature cutesy animal faces, while others boast punk-rock metal studs, chains, ball-separating straps, and hanging weights (see **ball stretchers**). A basic leather or Neoprene cock ring with adjustable snaps, Velcro, or D-rings is a great place to start. These are easy to don

even if you're already hard, you can experiment with different levels of constriction, and they can be removed faster than you can say, "My penis is turning purple!" (Sold everywhere; $.) Or try a plain rubber stretch cock ring for more simplicity ($; 1¾ inch diameter). They even come in glow-in-the-dark varieties! But the cock rings we get really excited about are those that are a little more *giving*. The Stretchy cock rings (WT sells a set of four for about ten bucks) feature little nubbins along the entire surface, which gently stimulate her clitoris. These rings are super-stretchy (hence the name), so the grip is pretty light, especially if he wears it around the shaft only.

Unfortunately, most of the super-stretchy cock rings out there contain **phthalates**—and it's not like you can whack a condom on a cock ring easily. (We actually tried covering one with Saran Wrap, but it was a disaster: Saran Wrap doesn't stretch.) So, here's what we suggest: **A-Womans-Touch.com** is the only store we know of that

R

uses a chemist to test *every* toy they sell for phthalate levels. Most of their toys are completely phthalate free, and some have very, very low levels of phthalates, but at a level that they, and their chemist, deem safe. So, if you're looking to invest in a mega-stretchy cock ring, stay safe and shop there.

rings, safe use of

Cock rings go on easiest when the penis is either flaccid or semierect. A bit of lube will help slide things along if it's not a snap-on ring, and you might want to trim the pubes around there, too, if he's particularly hirsute (especially if your ring has a Velcro attachment). If you're a newbie cock-ring user, *never use a solid ring*: Your cock ring should be either stretchy or should have a snap, Velcro, D-ring, or bolo-style closure. In fact, we're gonna go ahead and say you should have at least a decade of experience literally under your belt before experi-menting with something like BL's solid chrome Teardrop cock ring (almost $100!), stunning though it may be. In fact, GV is so against solid metal rings that it refuses to even carry them.

A cock ring should never be worn for more than twenty minutes at a time—and less than that if it starts to feel uncomfortable. Dude, you're trapping blood *in your penis*: Use a bit of common sense. If you ignored our advice (apparently it happens sometimes) and have a solid aluminum ring (BL) stuck on your swollen penis, try bringing down the erection with ice. If that doesn't do the trick, then get thee to the ER. Trust us—you won't be the first. Just cross your fingers that the hospital's metal cutters are strong enough that they won't have to call in the fire department for help. (*Oh, it happens.*)

rings, vibrating

Vibrating cock rings are built to hold a **miniature vibrator**. Vibrating clitoral stimulation

→

during intercourse? Now, *that's* sex the way Mother Nature intended it. Most of them are super-stretchy, though some are made of **leather** (like GV's Perfect Pair Ring; $$; vibe included). Unfortunately, like the stretchy cock rings with nubbins—see **rings, materials for**—most vibrating cock rings on the market contain **phthalates**. So, as with the nubbin cock rings, we suggest you shop for your stretchy vibrating cock rings at the phthalate-conscious **A-Womans-Touch.com** *only,* just to be safe. Their Blue Caress ($$, vibe included) is almost completely silent and covered in nubbins. Then there's their stretchy ring called Binky (illustrated; $$; vibe included), a super-squishy pink rabbit that takes a mini vibe through the head so his ears can stimulate your clitoris (what a guy). As long as you can get over the vision of a pink bunny gripping onto your man's penis like a koala bear (it *is* ridiculous looking, we admit), we predict O's all around. See also the PVibe in **high-end sex toys**, as well as **butterfly vibrators with harnesses**.

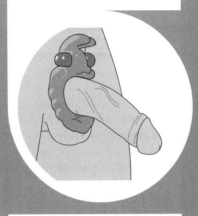

Ripple butt plug

This **butt plug** is **Tantus**'s biggest seller, and that's saying something once you know what else they stock. The Ripple comes in unassuming Small (5 inches by 1 inch) or slightly more impressive-slash-don't-bring-that-near-me Large (7 inches by 1½ inches). Kind of like **anal beads** disguised as a butt plug, it features four knuckle-like bumps along the stem, which feel particularly

R

nice as you move the plug in and out. Plus, the ripples allow you to insert the toy *very* gradually— a particularly encouraging partner might even cheer you on by saying, "Two knobs down, two to go!" Even better for beginners, the Ripple starts small and gradually widens toward the base, which gives you ample buildup time to breathe deeply and get used to that foreign object in your rectum. It's way sexier than it sounds, trust us. (GV's exclusive Spiral plug, $$, is a comparable product.) The Ripple is made of **silicone**, so it can be washed or boiled and should be used with a water-based **lube**. Available just about everywhere (MP calls it the Smooth Seducer)—Small is $, Large is $$. See also **P-spot**.

Rock Chick vibrator

At first glance, the Rock Chick looks a little scary, like a Grimace-colored clamp. But once you get it in your hands, all fear fades away. This U.K. import is made of nothing but super-supple, high-quality **silicone** that bends and gives. And, once you get it in your vagina, you realize how ergonomically designed it actually is. The U-shape simultaneously targets your **G-spot** (with the curved end) *and* your **clitoris** (with the ridged end). Simply use your palm to rock it back and forth to your liking—no awkward in-out thrusting necessary! Or, sit up or lie on your ➜

stomach to get your hips in on the rocking action. It even comes with a **bullet vibe** (with three watch batteries) that fits in the clitoral end; one touch of the protruding end of the bullet turns it on. Or use a free thumb to tap the bullet tip for a pulsating vibration. If you prefer to handle the clitoris yourself, you could turn the Rock Chick around and give your butt crack some vibration instead. Even women who don't love having their G stroked might *learn* to love it just because this toy is so cool.

Since the bullet's waterproof, you can take the whole thing in the shower. Remove the bullet to wash with hot water and soap, run through the dishwasher, or boil for a few minutes to truly sterilize it. Available for $$-$$$ (supercheap on BF!), which comes with water-based **lube**, toy cleaner, and **baby wipes**—sorry, "intimacy wipes."

rope (bondage or nylon)

A cheap, versatile, and readily available **restraint** for **BDSM** play. Soft, shiny, twisted (or braided) nylon is strong, comfortable, and nonchafing. It stays clean, it's long lasting, and it's easy to loosen (though maybe too easy in some cases). For a more rugged look and feel, try all-cotton clothesline—it's pliant and knots tightly (sometimes too tightly). Even better for a beginner is GV's Love Me Knots rope, a super-soft polyester-fiber cord that's safe on furniture and won't chafe or cut off circulation ($ for 9 feet). Whichever material you go with, get about 50 to 100 feet so you can cut it into several shorter pieces, varying from about 10 to 30 feet; shorter lengths are good for tying ankles and wrists together, and longer lengths work well for full-body binding. The thicker the rope, the less likely it is to cause circulation problems: Stick with something between 3/8 of an inch

R

and 1½ inches in diameter. For the tip of the safety-tips iceberg, see **restraints**; for more in-depth safety and technique info, check out Jay Wiseman's *The Erotic Bondage Handbook* or, if you can get your hands on a copy, *The Seductive Art of Japanese Bondage*.

rubber

See **latex rubber** and **jelly rubber**.

Ryder butt plug

This **butt plug** tends to have a little more staying power than the similarly sized **Buddy butt plug**. The Ryder is made by **Tantus** and is 4½ inches by 1½ inches. It's not tapered, so it might be a little harder to insert than Buddy, but its oblong base means it's less likely to pop out mid-sesh. The Ryder is **silicone**, so can be washed or boiled and should be used with a water-based **lube** (BF; $). See also **anal play** and **P-spot**.

S

safe, sane & consensual

A universally accepted credo of the **BDSM** community, though it should apply to *all* kinds of sex, even the most **vanilla**, toy-free sex. "Safe" means there's no risk of serious or permanent injury. "Sane" means that all parties involved are in control of themselves and interested in *mutual* pleasure. "Consensual" means that everyone has knowingly and voluntarily agreed to the sexual activities. See also the Safety Tips Appendix.

Saran Wrap

People used to use Saran Wrap for sexy mummification, especially in the **BDSM** community, but we're not quite sure how much of this has been going on since Kathy Bates tried it out on screen in 1991's *Fried Green*

→

Tomatoes. Great for making impromptu **dental dams**.

sensation play

Or should we say *sensational* play? Sex shouldn't always be rub, come, rinse, repeat. Add a little subtlety to your sexuality and you get *sensuality,* the driving force behind sensation play. It's notoriously been the domain of sensitive ponytailed men and earnest granola chicks who own speculums, but it doesn't have to be. No matter whether you have a sense of irony or not, experimenting with different textures and temperatures, both on and around your erogenous zones, wakes up your body to new experiences and surprises your nerves with the unexpected: the chill of an **ice** cube, the warmth of **candle wax**, the thud of a **paddle**, the pinch of a **nipple clamp**, the crack of a **riding crop** or **whip**, the tickle of feathers.

Heck, it might not even feel that good and you could still get off on it—that's one of the core principles of **BDSM**. Pain triggers the autonomic nervous system, which produces endorphins and increases your heart rate, breathing, and blood pressure—all of which is a lot like sex. This endorphin rush can enhance sexual pleasure and also make the pain feel less like discomfort and more like intense sensation. Just make sure safety comes first when you're dabbling with different sensations. (Race Bannon's *Learning the Ropes: A Basic Guide to Safe & Fun S/M Love-making* is a good place to start.)

sensitizing creams

Intended for clitorises that need to be hit over the head with a hammer, these ointments are supposed to increase sensation and therefore pleasure. But they may not be as effective or problem free as manufacturers would have you believe. Definitely don't use them internally. As far as topically on your clit goes, proceed with caution. The ingredients, like menthol, may make you feel tingly, may make you feel like there are fire ants in your pants, or may not cause much sensation at all, depending on the concentration and your reaction to it. All-natural minty toothpaste might work just as well (S/M people do it all the time). Some sensitizing balms also contain L-arginine, an enzyme that may encourage outbreaks in herpes sufferers. So, if you're sensitive down there or have herpes, it's better to just take the time to work some lube over and around your little chickpea—the attention alone should increase sensation! See also **desensitizing creams**, **penis** and **tightening creams**, **vaginal**.

sensory deprivation

Just as not deciding is a form of decision making, so sensory deprivation is a form of **sensation play**. Here's the idea: You limit one or more senses, and the others gets stronger. Limit

everything but touch, and your orgasm will feel like the center of the universe: **Blindfold** your partner, add **headphones** to restrict their ability to anticipate your touch, and maybe add **restraints** to limit their movement so the touching is all one way. We know, that's not quite *all* the senses—what do you think this is, Abu Ghraib?

sheets

Sex should always be a little dirty, but sometimes it's actually quite messy, too: on a heavy day of your period, when playing with food or chocolate, when using a lot of lube, when experimenting with female ejaculation, etc. Throwing caution to the wind is sexy and all, but what about those 700-thread-count sheets you just took out a second mortgage for? You could relocate to the **bath**, you could throw down a dark-colored towel, or you could use a waterproof sheet protector (available online or in the incontinence aisle at your local pharmacy or surgical

→

supply store). We know that shopping for sex props in the incontinence aisle is not the sexiest thing in the world, but maybe you're a bigger person than that. Maybe your vinyl sheets or absorbent mattress pad will even inspire a little saucy role-playing. Maybe Mommy is really, really mad that you wet the bed. Maybe someone deserves a good spanking.

Speaking of sheets, we'd like to take a brief moment to discuss satin sheets. We admit, it can feel pretty damn good to screw on satin, and we're all for a couple shopping together for satin sheets (and even if you don't particularly like the feel, there's just something about the concept that's hot). But most people would be highly suspicious if they went home with someone for the first time and discovered satin sheets on their new friend's bed—especially if those sheets were black. There's a fine line between sexy and cheesy, and if you choose to sleep on black satin on a regular basis—well, our dear friend, you have crossed it.

That said, sometimes something is so cheesy it's cool all over again. Like Sheets Gone Wild, by DamonAnthony.com ($$$$). These sateen cotton sheets are covered in illustrations of sexual positions to inspire you. But wait—there's more! The sheets are also an adult board game. We're not sure exactly how it works, but we're pretty sure there are no losers.

shops & shopping

See the introduction to this book.

silicone

An inorganic polymer. Or, better put, the safest soft material for anything you're going to insert in your bod—no contest. Here's the long list explaining why: There are no pores to harbor bad bacteria, you can put it in your dishwasher, you can sterilize it by boiling it in water or cleaning it with a 10 percent bleach

S

solution, you can swab it with alcohol, it's **phthalate** free, it's hypoallergenic, it's inert (so it won't react with other materials), it's long lasting, and it has little to no odor. Plus, silicone toys are often made by small companies that design them in house—they hand pour the molds in small batches to create effective, functional toys. For all these reasons, silicone toys cost more, but they're oh so worth it!

Make sure the product is advertised as *100 percent* silicone; otherwise, it may be mixed with **jelly** or other crappy material (sneaky bastards), nullifying all its kick-ass qualities. Keep it away from your cats; they love the feel of silicone, but one scratch and you'll have to donate it to their squeaky-toy collection for good. The only real bummer 'bout silicone is that, historically, manufacturers haven't been able to manipulate it into super-soft and super-funky textures like they can with **elastomers** and **jelly rubber**. But even that's changing with the invention of **VixSkin**, a lifelike material made from 100 percent boilable silicone.

Reputable silicone toy manufactuers include **Tantus**, **Vixen Creations**, and **Fun Factory** dildos. In general, silicone lubes should not be used with silicone toys, due to a weird chemical reaction, but see **lubes, silicone-based** for an exception to this rule.

Trivia tidbit: Silicon, the element, is often mistaken colloquially for silicone, as in the poignant pop classic "Objection (Tango)," where Shakira sings, "Next to her cheap *silicon* I look minimal" (lyrics off her official Web site). Though we like the sentiment, it should really be, "Next to her cheap *silicone* I look minimal." Class dismissed.

single-strap harnesses

—

See **harnesses**.

slappers

—

See **paddles**.

S

sleeves

❶ Masturbation aids for men to help simulate the feel of penetrating a vagina, anus, or mouth. For much more detail, see **masturbation sleeves**. ❷ Something you put over your penis or dildo to extend or texturize it. For much more detail, see penis **extenders**. A.k.a. **French ticklers**. ❸ Something you put over a toy, usually a smaller vibrator or **miniature vibrator** (like the **Pocket Rocket**, the Itty Bitty Vibe, or **bullet vibrator**), to give it a new shape and feel.

slimline vibrators

Old-school, missile-shaped, hard plastic **vibrators**—what most people picture when you say "sex toy." Some stores call them rockets; others, like **Good Vibrations**, refer to them as smoothies. Though we're grateful to be living in a time when a slimline is no longer the only option available, these vibes shouldn't be discounted entirely: They make a great **beginner toy** (due to their nonscary, familiar design), they're super cheap ($), they're low key (for times when your **Rabbit** is just too much bunny), and you can find them *everywhere* (even in the supersleazy sex shops we've tried our best to ignore in this book). Who says nostalgia isn't what it used to be? Some slimlines are waterproof (BL; $), some have variable vibe patterns like "escalating" and "staccato" (BF's Lime Rocket; $$), and some have a ribbed shaft for more interesting thrusting (MP's Pearl Rocket; $$). But the traditional slimlines are just this simple—6 inches →

S

long, just over 1 inch wide, and with two settings: On or Off. Plastic vibes are **nonporous**, are not safe for **anal play** (no flared base!), and can be wiped clean with a damp cloth.

slings, sex

Kind of like arm slings, except they wrap around the back of your neck and keep both your legs raised comfortably when you're lying in the receptive missionary position. Good for lazy bastards prone to cramps (BF; $$). Not to be confused with a sex **swing**.

Smartballs

Like **Ben Wa** and **duotone balls**, only smarter. The outer casing and the removal string are made of **Fun Factory**'s trademarked Elastomed—hard, nonporous, hypoallergenic, phthalate free—which makes them long lasting and a cinch to clean with warm water and mild soap. The package claims they stimulate, massage, and exercise the vagina; tighten up the vaginal muscles; support postnatal regenerative gymnastics (whatever that means); and help prevent incontinence. What, that's *it*? Plus, a patented manufacturing process makes Smartballs the quietest love balls in the world. In fact, they were so quiet, Lo forgot she had them in. After all, like any vaginal balls, the sensation is subtle, with a capital S. Still, their low-level sensation might be the perfect niggling to subconsciously get you ready for a hot date or simply brighten your day. But if you prefer your toys to club you over the head, try wearing them to a step class ($-$$; sold as Erotispheres on MP).

smoothies

See **slimline vibrators**.

softpacks

These are **dildos** that look and feel like real penises that women or transgendered folk can wear under their clothes and outside the bedroom—to a bar, say, or even just to the launderette. It's called softpacking or packing, and ladies who pack are sometimes referred to (not particularly creatively) as chicks with dicks. Unlike most dildos, softpacks tend to be flaccid, or semierect at the most (it's only polite, after all). Most of them are purely aesthetic—i.e., they're good for grabbing onto (and you'd be surprised what a realistic handful it makes through pants) but not fit for penetration.

Vixen Creation's Mr. Right ($$ on BF) is the best of the soft-packing bunch—it's made of VC's patented silicone **VixSkin**, which means it feels as lifelike as **Cyberskin** but is more durable and can be cleaned and sterilized like **silicone**. Mr. Right can be affixed with a packing strap ($ on VC) or a less bulky "cock sock" ($ on BL; GV calls them Packy Pockets), which is basically a jockstrap. Or, more simply, a pair of tight tighty-whities will hold him just as firmly. If Mr. Right gets sticky, just dust him with a little corn-starch (*not* talc, as it has been linked to cervical cancer). For a cheaper option, try one of the Softskin (see **Cyberskin**) soft-packs ($—price varies depending on size—at BL or GV). For a wearable dildo that you can actually use for penetration later in the evening, try VC's Tex—see **dildos, realistic**.

S

→

Finally, if you've always wanted to pee standing up, try one of GV's Mango Packers ($$$; peach or coffee colored): It's too floppy for penetration, but it does come with a built-in urinary device made of medical-grade latex. Yep, you can actually pee *through* your softpack! (Though it'll take a bit of at-home practice to get used to.) See also **bendable dildos & vibrators**.

Softskin

See **Cyberskin**.

spatula, kitchen

See **paddles**.

spreader bar

Be honest: Are you the kind of dirty bird who thinks "Hand-cuffs!" whenever you spy a set of nice, sturdy bars at the head of a bed? (A bed you're about to do it in, we mean, not your grandparents' classic sleigh bed—then again, you never know.) Do hospital beds just make you want to tie someone up with bedsheets? So, what happens when you fall in love with someone who sleeps on the futon? That's where the Bare Spread Bar comes in (BL; $$). It's made of black rubber for extra kink effect and is designed to spread someone's cuffed hands or feet—each end of the bar features a ring to attach a cuff to. Plus, you can easily attach other appendages to the bar with extra **restraints** for bent-over bliss. For a practical man's spreader bar, there's Under the Bed Restraints, made of lightweight, foldable, easily portable and hide-able nylon (BL; $$). See also **cuffs**, EB and EX.

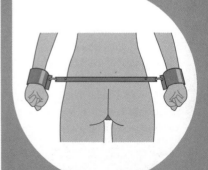

STDs

See the Safety Tips Appendix.

storage

Sex toys are like **condoms**: They're best kept in a cool, dry place. They're also best kept away from dust bunnies (especially the toys you put inside you—geez). And toys don't play well with other toys in storage—soft, squishy ones can melt into each other, hard toys can tear soft toys, **metal** toys can chip **glass** toys, heavy toys can dent impressionable ones, etc. Bear in mind that **Cyberskin** toys and their ilk "leak" pretty substantially, so don't store them among your nice undies, and don't leave them sitting on your antique dresser, either. Never ever put a toy away before it's completely dry. Dust Cyberskin (et al.) toys with cornstarch before storing them. Remove all batteries from toys when not in use (so they don't corrode inside or the toy

doesn't accidentally switch on and run them down). Remove all **miniature vibrators** from **dildos** and **butt plugs**.

The best (and cheapest) storage method we've heard yet is to take all those stray socks and put them to good use: One toy per sock, and you're done! If you don't have room in your nightstand, use shoeboxes under your bed for overflow storage. If you're prepared to invest a little, most sex shops sell cool lockboxes ($$) or washable, nylon-lined **Goody Bags**. Then there are the nifty Hide a Vibe Pillows (BF; BL calls them Treasure Pillows; $$): They look like regular throw pillows, but there's a secret zippered compartment, lined with silk, for storing all your sex toys and lubes. The concept is awesome, though we wish the fabric choices weren't jaguar, cougar, cheetah, leopard, or zebra. (What is it with the sex biz and animal prints?) Finally, if you have *way* too much time on your hands (a friend of ours actually did this for a beloved butt plug), you could go all prison chic and

→

build a secret hidey-hole inside a book by gluing the pages together and carving out a toy shape, just like Tim Robbins in *Shawshank Redemption*. See also **cleaning & care**.

strap-ons

When you take your **dildo** and put it in a **harness** so you can wear it like it's your very own dong, it's called a strap-on. When you fuck your girlfriend or boyfriend while wearing your strap-on, it's called strap-on sex. When a woman fucks her straight boyfriend up the butt with a strap-on, it's called disrupting the cosmic order, and it's a very good thing. See also **anal play**.

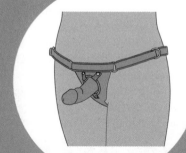

strap-on blow jobs

Not for everyone, to be sure. But maybe you've always wondered what it might feel like (in the head, at least) to get sucked off, or wanted your partner to experience *exactly* how hard it is to deep-throat, or just fancied saying, "Suck my dick!" and *meaning* it . . . . Or, on the other hand, maybe you've always wondered what it might feel like (in the head *and* in the mouth) to suck someone off. Well, with a **strap-on** you can make your dick dreams come true.

Sue Johanson's Royal Line

Canada's Dr. Ruth, Sue Johanson, took time out from her popular Oxygen call-in show *Talk Sex* to make her own line of waterproof, silicone-based thermoplastic rubber vibrators (produced by **California Exotics Novelties**). There are a bunch of models that appear to be ripped off

→

from **Fun Factory**, including several **dual-action** vibrators (like the **Rabbit**) with "one touch" activation, independent controls for reversible rotation and vibration, and an "EZ"-load battery pack (we didn't know it was that difficult before). Unfortunately, they're not 100 percent **silicone** (shame on Sue and Cal Exotics for not making that perfectly clear—even we got confused!), so you should use them with a condom, 'cause we have no idea what's in their "thermoplastic rubber." Fortunately, the manufacturers had the good sense to decorate the packaging with a cute little cartoon of Johanson rather than a seminaked photo, like they do with most of their toys. Visit Talksexwithsue.com/RoyalLine .html to order ($–$$$).

swings, sex

Contraptions, usually made of **leather** or nylon, attached via chains to the ceiling, that allow the rider to experience weightless sex in a number of positions that seem to defy physics and gravity ($$$$). Popular among the **BDSM** crowd, swingers, fisters, and apparently Pamela Anderson (at least during her Tommy days). Sometimes referred to as a sex **sling**. See also **erotic furniture**.

T

TantusSilicone.com

A leader in the **dildo**-manufacturing industry, right beside **Vixen Creations**. Makers of the patented **Feeldoe double dildos**, the **Bend Over Beginner Kit**, the slim **Ripple butt plug**, and the popular **Pro-Touch vibrating butt plug**, Tantus uses only 100 percent medical-grade **silicone**, so it's the safest material on the market (boilable, durable, hypoallergenic, easy to clean, and **phthalate** free!). Retailers say Tantus dildos and plugs, with their wide variety of shapes and colors, are always big sellers, though stores don't always advertise them as Tantus brand or use the manufacturer's name—so ask. You can even familiarize yourself with their extensive product line by sight on TantusSilicone.com, but, unfortunately, you can't order online from their less-than-kick-ass Web site.

Metis Black, their definitively kick-ass president, is committed to informing consumers, store clerks, and writers of sex-toy encyclopedias about the pros and the cons of various accessories and the **materials** they're made of—specifically, the pros of silicone dildos and the cons of everything else. (Sure, she's biased, but she's also right.) "People will stick almost anything up inside them because they're so ill informed," Black says. "Our manufacturing firm is based right outside San Diego, and the two biggest emergencies that come into the local hospital are husbands stabbed by their wives and men with inappropriate objects stuck up their butts—like *lightbulbs*!" See also **dildos, vibrating** and **Ryder butt plug**.

tea, hot

Take an oral sex break to sip from your steaming cup of chamomile. Don't ask why; just try it. (But don't stop to dunk a cookie—that's rude.) See also **sensation play**.

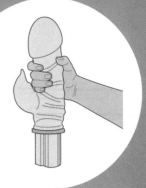

temperature play

See **ice**; **sensation play**; and **tea, hot**.

Terra Firma harness

See **harnesses, fixin's for** and **harnesses, materials for**.

Tex dildo

See **dildos, realistic**.

Thunder Cloud dual-action vibrator

We must admit, our main reason for including this **Vibratex** toy is that it cracks us up every time we look at it: The thing is huge! You're lucky if you can even get your hand around it (and some people consider that *really* lucky). And get this: Its shaft lights up in a flashing display of green, red, and blue when it's on the highest setting. Groovy, man. Design-wise, the Thunder Cloud is a cousin of the company's **Rabbit** series (rotating shaft plus clit tickler), though Vibratex admits it is their one toy that wasn't really built to complement the average female anatomy. In other words, it's for size queens: The bulbous head is 2⅜ inches across (almost twice the girth of the Rabbit) and the main shaft is 2 inches in diameter. The Thunder Cloud is made of Vibratex's new **phthalate**-free, **porous** material (mineral oil lends it a lifelike, **Cyberskin**-esque texture), so you need to use a (Magnum) **condom**

→

only if you're sharing or have a particularly sensitive vadge. Wash with soap and water and use with a water-based **lube**. Cheapest on DS ($$$$), it's also available on BL as Moby or GV as Twice as Titan for a few dollars more.

tightening creams, vaginal

Known in the vernacular as "pussy-tightening creams," these are right up there with vaginal **douching** and anal **desensitizers** in the bad-idea stakes: At *best* it will do nothing at all; at worst it might cause a yeast infection or else just numb the vagina—the idea being that if she can't feel anything, she's less likely to lubricate, and therefore her vagina will feel tighter. *Charming.* If you're really set on shaping things up down there, try **kegels** instead. And if your partner is really set on you trying one of these creams despite our warning, consider trading him in. See also **Xandria**.

Tingler, the

The closest you can get to sheer ecstasy without taking MDMH or having an orgasm. This cheap (DS; $) metal scalp-massaging tool is so simple—but then most ingenious ideas are. It looks kinda like a split-apart kitchen whisking tool. The Tingler gently touches acupressure points to send shivers throughout your entire body. And that's not just regurgitated marketing copy— that's for reals.

Toys in Babeland

See **Babeland.com**.

triple-action vibrators

Toys that stimulate a lady's clit, **G-spot**, and anus *at the same time,* such as the **Butterfly Effect wearable vibrator**. A.k.a. thrice-as-nice. See also **dual-action vibrators**.

Tristan Taormino

Tristan Taormino is the undisputed queen of anal sex. She is the author of a how-to book called *The Ultimate Guide to Anal Sex for Women* and the star of two adult videos based on that book, *The Ultimate Guide to Anal Sex I & II* (directed by the infamous John "Buttman" Stagliano and co-starring porn supah-star Nina Hartley). She even designed her own freakin' butt plugs, the Tristan and the **Tristan 2**. What have *you* done for butt sex lately, anyway? For more info, visit PuckerUp.com.

Tristan 2 butt plug

The silicone Tristan 2, a beer can of a **butt plug** at 4 inches by 2 inches, is designed by the Butt Queen herself, **Tristan Taormino**, in conjunction with **Vixen Creations**. The Tristan 2 even comes with a **miniature vibrator** that can be inserted into the core! (The original Tristan plug is "only" 3¾ inches by 1½ inches but doesn't vibrate.) A Tristan plug can be recognized by its particularly bulbous head and its rectangular base, which is designed to sit between the ass cheeks and make the plug easier to hold in place. It's made of **silicone**, so it can be washed or boiled. (Remove the vibe first!) Use with a *lot* of water-based **lube**. Available almost everywhere ($$).

T

"Tupperware" parties

Because most towns and cities in this country aren't blessed with

➔

a little sex-toy shop on the corner like **Good Vibrations** or **Babeland**, women are increasingly buying sex toys at Tupperware-style sex-toy parties, organized by companies like PassionParties.com and Safina.com. Don't be surprised if you're invited to a "Tupperware" party—wink, wink: A few years back, a Texas lady named Joanne Webb was arrested for hosting a Passion Parties event in Texas. Two undercover cops posed as a couple trying to spice up their sex life, and as soon as Joanne started explaining how to use a vibrator, they busted her. That's right, a sex-toy sting! Under Texas obscenity law, it's perfectly legal to sell sex toys as **novelties**, but it's a big no-no to suggest that the toys might actually get you off. Webb—a mother of three, a committed Baptist, and a former schoolteacher— was facing up to a year in jail until the charges were dropped.

If you're looking to stay on the right side of the law, the three U.S. states with restrictions on sex-toy sales are Texas, Alabama, and Georgia. In all three states,

sex toys may be sold for "educational" or "novelty" purposes only. Some stores in these states may make you sign an affidavit swearing you won't be doing any sinning with your purchase. We guess that whole "pursuit of happiness" thing holds true only if you can get to your happy place just by thinking about it (though even then, you're still probably going to hell).

tweezers clamps

See **nipple clamps**.

U

Ultraskin

See **Cyberskin**.

undercover toys

Looks like a pump, feels like a sneaker? How about looks like a lipstick, feels like oh oh ohhh OHHH YES YES YES YES YES!!! Undercover toys are the Southern sorority girls of the sex-toy world: They look all innocent on the outside, but they're secretly totally slutty. There's the lipstick vibe (GV calls it the Purse Pal; $), the nail polish vibe (MP; $$), the mascara vibe (BL; $$), the VibraPen (BL; $$), the vibrating hairbrush (BL; $), the rubber **Duckie**, and the vibrating sponge and shower scrunchie (see **bath accessories**)—all everyday household items that just happen to vibrate. (And we all know what we do with things that just happen to vibrate.) None of these vibrators is particularly sophisticated or sturdy—it's approximately the same idea as holding your electric toothbrush down there—but that's not the point, damn it. You're paying for the gimmick more than for a good vibration.

Pop an undercover toy into your wash kit before a business trip, into your pocketbook before a tough day at work, or even into your pocket before a night on the town with your beau (surprise him or her by slipping it into their pants under the table at the bar). Consider it your secret weapon—just like James Bond, except without all the killing and misogyny.

Undercover toys also make great gifts. A less-than-enlightened woman might take offense at receiving a **Rabbit** for her b-day, but a novelty vibe can be accepted "in jest" and then experimented with later in secret. Hey, if it takes a battery-operated "pen" to convert a nonbeliever, we'll all for it.

See the Toy Guide for a comprehensive list of undercover toys featured in this book.

V

vacuum cleaner

Not a sex toy. Don't stick your dick in it or your clit on it. You might think this is obvious, but you'd be surprised.

vagina, artificial

See **masturbation sleeves**. A.k.a. pocket pussy.

vaginal canal

The vagina is kind of like the perfect studio apartment—there's a whole lot more room in there than you'd think. The back two-thirds of the vagina can actually double in size during arousal. (*Now* do you understand fisting?) The front third of the vagina, however, swells and *tightens* during arousal. And it's this front third where most of the nerve endings live. (*Now* do you understand the **Rabbit**'s pearls?) The **G-spot** is usually in (or around) this neighborhood, too—it's the spongy area on the upper wall, about 2 inches inside. Women can feel *pressure* in the back two-thirds of their vagina, of course, but there's really not a lot of sensitivity back there (though getting your cervix—the door to the uterus at the far end of the canal—slammed may not feel so hot). So, size doesn't really matter, you see—at least, not length. Curves and girth are usually more important. That's why so many of the innie toys in this book look fairly insubstantial to an untrained eye: They've actually been designed with a woman's anatomy in mind. Shocking, we know.

By the way, you might have heard people talk about another area of the woman's vagina, sometimes called the T-Zone or the A-Zone or (less jauntily) the anterior fornix: This is another area that can be massaged through the upper wall of the vagina, except much farther

→

→ inside—as deep as, or sometimes deeper than (i.e. *past*, not through), the tip of the cervix. Some women say they actually prefer this to G-spot stimulation, and, as we explain in the **pelvic floor muscles** entry, everything is so interconnected down there that there's no reason why it shouldn't. The only thing that really matters is getting in there and figuring out what, exactly, you like the most, and where, exactly, you like it. Once you find the spot(s), you can call it whatever the hell you want! See also **clitoris**.

vanilla

The opposite of kink. If the most "experimental" thing you've ever done in bed is leave the light on, you are decidedly vanilla. Vanilla, however, is a relative concept. If, for example, you consider **BDSM** a lifestyle choice and like to be peed on as foreplay, you might call someone "vanilla" for choosing a cute little **paddle** over a 10-foot bullwhip. There's nothing wrong with feeling a little vanilla—it just means you haven't tried all thirty-one flavors yet. Nor is there anything wrong with never wanting to try *all* thirty-one flavors—not everyone likes peanut-butter swirl. It's not vanilla to veto the occasional act, as long as you're open to what turns your partner on and promise not to laugh when they confess their deepest, darkest fetish. What vanilla is *not* is a synonym for *normal*. Normal sex is a concept that exists only in the minds of right-wing extremists. (Actually, screw that—in the darkest corners of their minds, they're probably the kinkiest bastards around.) "Normal" is what you want your doctor to say about that big, hairy mole or what you want your pilot to say about the turbulence. **Good Vibrations** actually sells a Vanilla Bondage Kit, a kind of on-ramp into the world of BDSM-lite accessories: a comfortable, adjustable, silk **blindfold** and two silk ties (2½ feet long each) come in an ice cream container ($).

vegetarian & vegan toys

If you're a veg-head, it's hard enough trying to find products with no animal parts or by-products to stick in your mouth, let alone your lower body cavities. But there are a couple places specializing in animal-friendly kink: VeganErotica.com and VegSexShop.com. Plus, general sex shop Early2Bed.com has a special vegan category in its navigation bar.

Vibra-Exciter Cell Phone vibrator

A sort of **undercover/remote control toy** hybrid from Vibrafun. It's a silver plastic **bullet** vibe attached by a cord to a battery pack in the shape of a small, cheap, fake cell phone that clips to your belt. The vibe is actually activated by your *real* cell phone: When you get a call (or when any phone within 3 feet

of you receives a call, for that matter), the vibe action lasts for the duration of the call, and when you (or anyone near you) get a text, it lasts thirty seconds—same goes for when you *make* a call or text. Great for planned phone-sex seshes. Just make sure your calling plan has lots of free minutes. If you fear you might go over your minutes, you can also use the vibe manually. (BL; $$; two AAA batteries.)

Vibratex

Best known as the maker of the **Rabbit Habit & Rabbit Pearl vibrators** and the importer

→

of the **Hitachi Magic Wand**, manufacturer and distributor Vibratex was the first company to bring **dual-action** vibrators to North America. Before that, it was just missile-style and realistic-looking vibes with the knob on the bottom of the shaft; none had a separate motor for clitoral stimulation. A small, family-owned company prizing quality over quantity (much like **Tantus** and **Vixen Creations**), Vibratex strives to design products that complement a woman's anatomy, won't break down after three uses, and are made in Japan from high-quality material (well, about as high quality as you can get when you don't use silicone). They use nonsilicone **elastomers** that can be molded into various textures more easily. That means all Vibratex products are porous, and many of the oldie but goodies (like the Rabbit) contain **phthalates**.

However, unlike cheaper brands, Vibratex toys aren't nearly as toxic: They don't reek and are much less porous. (Even **A-Womans-Touch.com** sells them, so you know they're

on the safe side.) And they've got a new line of toys made of 100 percent phthalate-free and latex-free elastomer! (See the **Rabbit Habit & Rabbit Pearl vibrators** entry for examples.) Though you don't need to worry about toxins seeping out with those, bacteria could still seep *in,* so **condom** use is suggested if you've got a sensitive vagina and *highly* recommended if you're sharing. They also make the popular Water Dancer vibrator (see **Pocket Rocket**). Though there are certainly more high-tech **dual-action** vibes out there—like **California Exotics Novelties**'s Chinese-made Jack Rabbit with LED indicator, glow-in-the-dark push buttons, and seemingly infinite combinations of rotation, vibration, and pulsing patterns—they can't compare to Vibratex's superior production and material. (Tech geeks beware: As wicked cool as the Jack Rabbit sounds—and kind of is—it's unbearably sticky and literally stinks!)

V

vibrating panties

See **remote control toys**.

vibrators, about

Sex-toy newbies often get confused when they first see a vibrator like the **Hitachi Magic Wand**. "But where does it go in?" they ask concernedly. (In case you don't read on: It doesn't.) Here's the thing: The majority of vibrators (at least, the ones that really care) are designed to stimulate the **clitoris**, first and foremost. And, as we all know, though the clit runs deep, its most sensitive nubbin lives just north of the entrance to the vagina. Sure, there are some nerve endings in the **vaginal canal**—most of them in the outer third—but it's the clit that responds most dramatically to good vibrations. And when we say "dramatically," we mean it. Many, many, many, many, *many* women learn to achieve orgasm using a vibrator, and some women can only ever get there with a little help from their buzzy friends (for the record, there's no shame in that; see **addiction**). And we have yet to meet a sex educator who *wouldn't* encourage a woman to enlist the help of a vibe to reach her happy place. Even Dr. Ruth says so—see the **Eroscillator** she endorses.

Don't think of the vibrator as a replacement for a penis; think of it as an extension of your hand. Take the toy wherever your hand likes to roam: thighs, mons, labia, clitoris. (If your hand likes to roam inside, make sure you pick a vibe that can safely go there—see following.) You may find that holding the vibrator directly over your

→

clit is too much—the clit is a sensitive little bugger like that. Start with the lowest setting on your toy (if it has options), move it to your mons or labes (your clit will still benefit from the vibes), or hold it over a pillow or blanket to help disperse more mellow vibes throughout your genital region. Experiment with moving it around or keeping it in one place. Tease yourself with it—or hand the toy over to your partner and let *them* tease *you*.

By the way, external vibration isn't just for females: A guy might enjoy running a vibe up and down the shaft of his penis, too, or pressing into his **perineum** (it's a baby step toward a vibrating **butt plug**!). If you want to keep using the toy throughout intercourse (like we said, there's no shame in it), rear-entry or woman-on-top positions work best. However, if the penis or dildo owner dons a vibrating cock **ring**, you can do it however the hell you want! Go nuts and do it missionary style!

Here's the basic difference between a vibrator and a **dildo**:

A dildo, by definition, always goes in somewhere (given enough lube and patience); a vibrator doesn't necessarily— though some do. So, the first question you have to answer when picking a vibe is, innie or outie? Am I looking for internal stimulation, external stimulation, or a bit of both?

Vibrators may turn you into a reverse size-ist: That honking **Hitachi** might be okay company when it's just you, but it doesn't make for the sexiest three-way when your partner's in town. Diminutive vibes like the **Pocket Rocket** or a **miniature vibrator** are less likely to be a buzz kill (as it were). Consider whether you'll be using a toy solo or with company before making your purchase— and, if you're in the store, turn it on to hear and feel it. Smaller vibes are typically quieter and buzz less vigorously, though there's not always a direct correlation. For example, all **Fun Factory** toys—even the biggest ones—are quiet as a mouse, and yet they all buzz with zeal, too. Others, like the **Eroscillator**,

V

shimmy more like an electric toothbrush. (See the individual toy descriptions in this book for more details.) **Good Vibrations** also offers a handy chart comparing toys' volume and intensity. Hint: A noisy toy can be drowned out by cranking up your **iPod**.

You may have noticed that throughout this book, *vibrating* is used as an adjective in front of names of toys that wouldn't traditionally be classified as vibrators. You've got your vibrating cock **rings**, your vibrating **finger toys** like the **Fukuoku 9000 finger toy**, your vibrating **butt plugs**, your vibrating **dildos**, your vibrating **nipple clamps**, your vibrating penis **sleeves**, your vibrating **harnesses**, and your vibrating penis cups (see **boy toys**). Most of these employ the help of a **miniature vibrator**, which is inserted into, or strapped onto, the toy.

Finally, a quick safety note: Never use your vibrator on unexplained calf pain. See the Safety Tips Appendix for an explanation, as well as a discussion of the rumors surrounding nerve damage and vibe use. (Don't panic; there's no bad news.)

There are more kinds of vibes than kinds of shrimp. See the Toy Guide for vibes featured in this book, grouped by category.

vibrators, battery-powered

Most vibes are battery operated—it's pretty much just the **Eroscillator** and the **"back" massagers** like the **Hitachi Magic Wand** and the **Wahl vibrator** that plug into an outlet. Plug-in toys last longer and tend to be more powerful than their battery-operated kin, but you typically can't put them inside you, you can't take them in water, and you can't take them more than a few feet from an outlet. The latest development in this field is **rechargeable** sex toys. Some battery-operated toys, like the **Rabbit Pearl**, come

➔

with control switches on the battery packs, which can be fun for your partner to play with when the vibe is inside you. Others even come with a **remote control** so your partner can tease you from across the room. Battery vibes (and the batteries themselves) will last longer if you remove the batteries when the toy is not in use. If your battery toy has a cord, never pull on it. And don't lie on or fall asleep on a buzzing toy–those babies get hot! For info on watch batteries, see **miniature vibrators**.

vibrators, external

Sometimes called outies, vibrators that are built purely for external stimulation (i.e., the clit and labia) include the **Duckie waterproof vibrator**, the **Eroscillator**, the **Hitachi Magic Wand**, the **Laya Spot**, the **Lelo vibrators**, **Pure Bliss**, the **Wahl vibrator**, the vibrating sponge (see **bath accessories**), any **novelties**, **finger toys**, or

miniature vibrators, and anything marketed as a **"back" massager**. However, the Eroscillator, the Hitachi, and the Wahl can all be converted into innies with the help of specially designed attachments.

vibrators, internal

Sometimes called innies, vibrators that are designed specifically for internal stimulation. They may have girth or beads to focus on the opening, gyration for the internal edges of the vaginal canal, a curve or hook to target a favorite spot like the **G-spot**, or some combination thereof (see **Rabbit Habit & Rabbit Pearl vibrators**). Note: Many sites and stores are annoyingly vague about whether a vibe is safe to use internally. A safe rule of thumb is, if the packaging doesn't explicitly say that it's safe to use as an innie, assume it's external-use only (or ask a friendly sales assistant for help). See also **dildos, vibrating**.

vibrators, multitasking

Multitasking toys provide both internal and external vibration *simultaneously*. The most common are **dual-action** vibrators, which stimulate the clitoris and inside the vagina. Not content with this double-action, **triple-action** vibes take it up one more notch, meaning they stimulate the back door, too.

vibrators, switch-hitting

Switch hitters are vibrators that can be either internal or external, depending on your mood. These include the **Aqua Arouser waterproof vibrator**, the **Clitoral Hummer waterproof vibrator**, the **Cosmic vibrator**, **Fun Factory**'s silicone Patchy Paul (called the Heartbreaker vibrator at BL, $$), and **slimline vibrators**. Basically, the insertable part of any innie vibe should be waterproof, it

shouldn't have any sharp edges or potentially irritating knobs and seams, and, if it's going up the butt, it should have a flared base so it doesn't get lost up there. (If it's going in the veegee only, then it doesn't need a flared base, but it shouldn't be so diminutive that it could get lost up there—like, say, a **miniature vibrator**.)

vinyl

A material often associated with and used by the **BDSM** community. Sometimes referred to as PVC (short for polyvinyl chloride), though not all vinyl is PVC (we know, it confuses the hell out of us, too). Vinyl is a widely used plastic that is durable, inexpensive, and easily manufactured but can cause serious pollution in its production, often has additives (like **phthalates**) that can leak, and cannot be readily recycled. (Greenpeace is pulling for a PVC-free future.) Most soft and flexible vinyl products will contain phthalates, though they're

→

probably better for you than **jelly rubber** toys, since they're not as porous. Generally, vinyl feels firmer than jelly, it lasts longer than jelly (but not as long as **silicone**), and is less expensive than silicone.

Since it's porous, the only way to keep vinyl toys clean and bacteria free is to use condoms over them; plus, you'll be reducing your exposure to possibly harmful phthalates and making cleanup a cinch in the process. But if you know it's a higher-quality vinyl than most (e.g., all **Vibratex** vinyl products, like the **Rabbit**, are made of food-grade vinyl, and all vinyl products at **A-Womans-Touch.com** have been tested and considered safe), if you make it a **monogamous toy**, and if you clean it properly, **condoms** may not be necessary (especially if it's just used externally). To wash the actual toy, use a damp, soapy cloth (mild soap is best). Examples include some of the **Hitachi Magic Wand attachments** and the spongy head of the Wand.

Vixen Creations.com

Whatever you do, don't call their dildos "**novelties**." More like "works of art." After all, the ladies at this small but exceptional manufacturer take pride in what they do: They hand make all their dildos and butt plugs out of 100 percent premium **silicone** and offer a lifetime guarantee on each (we don't know anyone else who does that). The founder, Marilyn Bishara, used to work at **Good Vibrations** and saw that no one could supply silicone dildos fast enough—so she pounced on the opportunity, launching Vixen Creations (so called "because a female fox does not take shit from anyone"). Unlike **Tantus**, the other leader in primo pokers, Vixen sells their products to the public on their Web site, VixenCreations.com, often at significantly lower costs than the general retailers do. For descriptions of some of their best-selling products, see **Buddy butt plug**, **Nexus double dildos**, and **Tristan 2 butt plug**. Other popular Vixen products are discussed in **dildos, realistic**; **dildos, nonrealistic**; **dildos, size**; **Hitachi Magic Wand attachments**; and **softpacks**.

VixSkin

A new miracle **material** created by the wonderful women of **VixenCreations.com**: It's realistically fleshy like **Cyberskin et al.**, but somehow it's 100 percent **silicone**! That means it's **nonporous**, **latex** free, boilable, and won't degrade or break down in quality, unlike most **softpacks**, the **Fleshlight**, and other **masturbation sleeves**. Plus, it's **phthalate** free. We haven't heard good news like this since we saved a bunch of money on our car insurance. Use either a high-quality, *pure* silicone lube *without* additives like Eros Gel (see **lubes, silicone-based**) or any water-based lube, such a Liquid Silk. Check out the Mr. Right softpack and Tex dildo at VC. See also **dildos, realistic**.

vulva puppet

Handmade satin pillows of the female genitalia made by House O' Chicks that educate about anatomy, glorify goddess power, and give people second-hand embarrassment.

W

Wahl vibrator

Sometimes called the Wahl 7-in-1 or the Wahl Coil, the Wahl is second only to the **Hitachi Magic Wand** in the wink-wink, nudge-nudge, "no, really, it's a **'back' massager**" charade. The Wahl is coil operated, which means it's lighter, faster, and *waaay* quieter than the Hitachi. Like the Hitachi, a Wahl can last for years if you treat it right. Officially, according to Wahl (and if you talk to our lawyer, this is what you heard from us), it's not supposed to be used on the genitals—it even says so in the manual. Unofficially, well, women have been using it on their happy place for years, and responsible stores like BF, BL, and GV continue to stock it, so we feel pretty good about turning a blind eye. (WT sells it but cautions against genital use—*riiiight.*)

According to Carol Queen, GV's staff sexologist, "The Wahl Clipper corporation apparently had a Catholic priest on their board of directors, and the 'genitals' warning reflects the cultural image he wanted to portray. The company knows damn good and well what we sell these vibrators for, and they seem perfectly happy to continue to supply us." Then again, Wahl told the ladies at **A-Womans-Touch.com** that some people have reported injuries after using their massager downtown, so proceed at your own risk.

The Wahl looks kind of like a handheld blender, and comes with a bunch of attachments for "scalp massage," "deep

→

muscle massage," "spot application massage," etc. The spot tool is best suited for external clitoral stimulation, though we'd like to add that the scalp tool gives a damn good scalp massage, too. (Hey, there's only so much clitoral vibration a woman can take in a day.)

One downside is that holding the Wahl for an extended period can make your hand go numb. If you find that particularly annoying, check out the comparable Essential Massager (see **"back" massagers**)—it's less numbing, though it isn't as quiet as the Wahl. (The Essential's warning simply says not to use on "sensitive skin," FYI.) The Wahl is for external use only—if you want to make it an innie vibrator (see **vibrators, internal**), see **Wahl attachments**. Made of hard plastic, so it can be wiped down with a damp soapy cloth. (Unplug it first, Einstein.) The Wahl is available all over for $-$$, depending on the model and number of attachments. See also **Berman Center Intimate Accessories**.

Wahl attachments

Anywhere that sells the **Wahl vibrator** will typically also stock Wahl attachments that turn your external **vibrator** into an innie, either regular (i.e., straight) or **G-spot** (i.e., curved). These are mostly made of **vinyl** and run about ten bucks a pop. For boys, you can buy a tulip-shaped attachment to fit around the head of the penis for a few dollars less: It's called the Hugger Attachment at BL and the slightly unsavory-sounding Come Cup Attachment at GV; it's available at WT as the Cup Attachment. Use **condoms** with 'em for safety.

Water Dancer vibrator

See **Pocket Rocket vibrator**.

whipped cream

See **edible accessories**.

waterproof toys

Toys aren't just for the bedroom—they make great shower-time companions, too. There are a buttload of waterproof props out there (see the Toy Guide for a list of ones featured in this book). Or, make any small battery-operated vibrator waterproof by putting it in a condom and knotting the end. By the way, if something is described as water resistant or splash proof, that's not the same thing as waterproof. Even with water-proof vibes, always make sure their battery compartments are tightly sealed and kept dry inside. Don't forget that show-ering will rinse away your natu-ral lube, as well as water-based **lubes**. Try a silicone-based lube for a little more underwater staying power.

whips

Just the thought of whipping real good, à la Devo, makes a lot of people want to curl up in sweats and rent a Julia Roberts flick. But if either **sensation play** or **BDSM** is your thing, whips can really turn it up to eleven. For those in the BDSM community, the bullwhip—their nickname for a single-tail whip—is something of a holy grail (see StormyLeather.com for a selection—and be prepared to drop a couple hundred). Enthusiasts (see Bullwhip.org) rave about the "pop" noise the tip of the whip makes as it moves through the air (even going so far as to claim that this is a result of breaking the sound barrier—yes, serious BDSM play seems to attract its share of science geeks). However, we must insist that you attend a

→

how-to seminar before even *considering* using something as hardcore as a bullwhip at home (even if you've been whipping actual bulls all your life). Sex shops often offer classes—ask your friendly sales rep if they can recommend one.

Significantly less hard-core than the bullwhip is the **flogger**: Rather than a single tail, this consists of a whole bunch of much shorter tails—typically wide, flat strips of leather—attached to a handle (available everywhere for $$; try the BARE products at BL). A flogger delivers more of a thud than a sting, though it should nevertheless be wielded with care: A human tushy is a sensitive bruise-able pear, and we shudder at the damage that could be done to someone's genitals by a clumsily wielded whip. Browse Tes.org and Sexuality.org or pick up a copy of Joseph W. Bean's book *Flogging* if you want to learn more.

But what if you just want to turn it up to, like, ten and a half? Why not try a starter whip like BL's Red Mini Whip ($): It's made up of hundreds of rubber spaghetti-esque strands that offer a light, stingy sensation. BF sells a similar product called, rather prosaically, the Thin Rubber Whip; MP calls theirs the Velvet Tantalizer. But even with cute whips like these in cheery primary colors, you should apply with caution. (If you were ever rat-tailed at summer camp, you know what we're talking about.) Build up slowly, avoid the face and genitals, and play nice. And remember: You can leave your Devo hat on.

A-Womans-Touch.com (WT)

A-Womans-Touch.com is a little pocket of integrity in the sex biz. Of course, every store recommended in this book has integrity to spare (that's why we picked 'em—duh) but WT in particular takes its sex-ed role *very* seriously. Check it out: They don't even stock **jelly** toys, because of the **phthalates** issue! In fact, they work with a chemist who tests *every freakin' toy* they stock for phthalate levels! (Their chemist also tests for **latex**, which will be good news to all those who are allergic to it.) Most of the toys WT sells are completely phthalate free—the rest have super-low levels of phthalates and don't contain any of the top ten most dangerous kinds of phthalates, so the chemist (and WT) considers them safe to use.

It shouldn't be surprising to learn the company is based in Madison, Wisconsin (where everyone's so freakin' nice and *concerned*).

Their flagship store is in Madison, and they're about to open another bricks-'n'-mortar store in Milwaukee (if they haven't already). WT likes to replace the manufacturers' off-putting, cheesy packaging with their own discreet bags to make customers feel more comfortable with their purchase. The staff all bring their dogs to work. And, most nobly, they are committed to finding and selling toys that address sexual dysfunction or changes due to illness, disability, or aging. The business is run by founder Ellen Barnard and her friend, a physician; their extended staff is trained to answer questions on everything from orgasmic function and erectile dysfunction to postmenopause or even postcancer sex. They're such good souls that it would be downright evil to mock their earnestness (or their stated fondness for hugging). So all we can say is, we love you, A-Womans-Touch.com!

X

X-rated

Something that *did,* in fact, mean to turn you on (though there's no guarantee that it will).

Xandria

Oh, Xandria, why all the purple? Does it really make people want to buy more sex toys? You probably know Xandria's name from those ads in the back of magazines like the *New Yorker* and *Harper's*: They've been around for thirty years (second oldest in the biz, after AdamandEve .com) and are able to advertise in "upstanding" pubs because they don't sell pornos (only *instructional* videos). They're not the most sensitive or enlightened of sex-toy outlets, however—the last time we logged on, they were pushing Oh So Tight pussy-**tightening cream** (for that "snug-like-a-

virgin feeling") on their home page. And the customer reviews often veer into Penthouse Forum territory. But it's a worthwhile stop-off if you're price shopping, and they do have a very nice return policy: You can return an item for any reason and get a replacement, a substitution, or even a refund. So, just in case you decide to ignore our two-thumbs-down and order that Oh So Tight anyway, they've got you covered. Now, go do sixty **kegels** as penance.

Z

Zzzzzzzzz

❶ The sound of a little love motor. ❷ The sleepy sigh of satisfaction you'll be making after you find—and play with— your perfect toy.

Safety Tips Appendix

Here are the twenty golden rules of playing safe with toys. Learn them, live them, love them.

1. Always **clean** a toy right after using it and let it dry thoroughly before putting it away.

2. **Store** your toys with care, and they'll last much longer. Plus, if you don't store a toy properly, you'll have to clean it again before using it.

3. Know what **material** your toy is made of so you know how to clean it and what **lube** to use it with. If you don't know what material your toy is made of, call up the company that made it and demand to know *all* the ingredients (we, the consumers, are the ones who will make this industry safer). If you can't get a straight answer or don't trust the answer you're given (even the conscientious retailers don't always know for sure), play it safe and put a **condom** on it.

4a. While most STDs can't live outside the body for very long, the warm and moist environment of an in-use sex toy can harbor bacteria or viruses long enough for you to say "Pass the dildo, baby." So yes, you *can* get (or give) an STD from a shared sex toy. Even if you let hours pass before it's swapped, there's no way for you to tell what harmful bacteria still might be hanging around. So always put a **condom** on it (one per person per use), unless you're sure the toy is 100 percent **nonporous** and can therefore be completey sterilized between uses by different individuals. Even if you are putting on a fresh condom before each swap, we'd recommend washing the toy between condom changes, too, just to be on the safe side.

4b. Know the difference between **porous** and **nonporous**.

5. Never use vibrators on unexplained calf pain. (Random, we know—it's because of the danger of dislodging a blood clot that might be causing said pain.)

6. Know what **phthalates** are. If a low-quality toy is seeping phthalates (i.e., it's sticky and smells up a room), always use it with a condom, a **latex glove**, or a **dental dam**, even if it's a monogamous toy.

7. If you can see shit growing on it, don't stick it inside you. But know this: You can't always see the shit that might be growing on it. Even if your porous toy is phthalate free and monogamous, it can still harbor bacteria if you don't **clean** it properly (which could cause a yeast infection, etc). See rules 1 and 2. And if you have a particularly sensitive vagina, consider using a condom even with *monogamous* porous toys.

8. A sex toy should never be moved from an ass to a vagina without changing condoms or sterilizing it first, unless you're prepared for a nasty bacterial infection.

9. Buy your sex toys from one of the shops or manufacturers recommended in this book. There are some sleazy toy retailers out there, and you shouldn't trust them with either your genitals or your credit card information.

10. If a toy comes with instructions, read them (however, see also rule 20). If it doesn't, ask/e-mail a sales rep to explain the toy to you. If no one will help you, you're shopping in the wrong place.

11. Never put talc on your toys to dry them; it's been linked to cervical cancer. Use cornstarch instead.

12. Never stick something up your **butt** that doesn't have a flared base.

13. If you're going to leave a toy in all day, you better be 110 percent sure it's nonporous and sterilized. But we don't

recommend using a toy for more than a few hours at a time.

14. If you're planning on dabbling in **BDSM** or serious **sensation play**, do your research first. (This book doesn't count.)

15. If you're allergic to **latex**, use a polyurethane condom over any toy that you're not 110 percent sure is latex free. *Many* sex toys contain latex, and the packaging isn't always particularly clear on this fact (again, see rule 20).

16. We love toys that come with a guarantee, and so should you! Of course, a guarantee is moot if you're too embarrassed to return a faulty toy. Get over it.

17. A high price tag doesn't always guarantee high quality. But anything with a price tag so low that it's too good to be true, probably is.

18. Never try to fix a sex toy yourself. If it has protruding wires or is on the fritz, throw it out and start over.

19. Rumors abound that vibrators can cause permanent nerve damage. Okay, so, yes, there is a *teeny-tiny* chance this could happen—just as it could happen with your fingers, too. But it's very, *very* rare. "We have only seen this in instances of severe alcohol or drug abuse," says Carol Queen, GV's staff sexologist. "In a situation like this, the user's judgment is clouded and their ability to feel is compromised; this isn't how most people use toys or masturbate by hand." So, there you go: Friends don't let friends diddle drunk. Tipsy is fine (and often a fabulous idea, now that we think about it); shitfaced is not. By the way, your genitals might feel *temporarily* numb after using a particularly strong vibe or pressing down hard with a buzzing toy. If this is the case, you could try a toy with a more subtle vibe, or use your vibrator over a blanket or jeans.

20. Always trust your instincts. The sex-toy industry is not regulated, which means labels are often unintentionally confusing or even intentionally misleading. If something gives you a rash or feels uncomfortable or doesn't look safe to put inside you or just plain feels wrong, then stop—even if this book said it was okay.

Toy Guide